DANGEROUS PLACES

For Jane Danver, orphaned and alone in Danver Hall, there was danger everywhere...

... in the ruined west wing of the manor, where her parents met death so many years ago...

... in the hidden stairway to the tower, where Jane had almost met her doom...

... in the outlying cottage where the beautiful girl who was Jane's only friend played a strange game of passion with the man Jane loved...

... in the powerful arms of handsome, dissolute Brence Danver, for whom Jane was a plaything to be broken and tossed away....

But Jane knew where the greatest danger lay—in the secret depths of her own mind, where unspeakable horror lay concealed like a fatal trap waiting to be sprung....

JAMINTHA

Beatrice Parker

A DELL BOOK

Published by
DELL PUBLISHING CO., INC.
1 Dag Hammarskjold Plaza
New York, New York 10017

Copyright © 1975 by Tom Huff

All rights reserved. No part of this book
may be reproduced in any form or by any means without
the prior written permission of the Publisher,
excepting brief quotes used in connection with
reviews written specifically for inclusion in a
magazine or newspaper.

Dell ® TM 681510, Dell Publishing Co., Inc.
Printed in the United States of America
First printing—February 1975

CHAPTER ONE

I tried to banish the apprehension. There was no reason to feel this way, no reason at all, yet the nervous uneasiness remained as the ancient coach rattled over the rough terrain, bringing me nearer and nearer to Danmoor. I was the only passenger. A lumpy burlap bag filled with mail occupied the seat across from me. Danmoor was remote, isolated on the edge of the moors, and the mail coach made but one trip a week. I had been fortunate to make the connection. Clutching the edge of the seat to lessen the joggling, I stared out the windows at the desolate countryside, bleak gray and brown with patches of tarry black bog and a few gnarled green trees. It was like the rim of the world, barren, disturbing, filled with menace.

I couldn't believe this was really happening. A month ago I had graduated at the head of my class. The boarding school was austere and strict, but it had been home to me for eleven long years. My uncle had provided the money, true, but I had had no communication with him during all that time. He was a complete stranger. I had assumed I would find some sort of employment after graduation, and the summons had come as a complete surprise: "Expecting you at Danver Hall September 12. Fare enclosed. Charles Danver." That was all, and now I was on my way to a house I could not remember.

Even though I had spent the first seven years of my life there, Danver Hall remained shrouded in mist in my memory. I could not recall it, no matter how hard I concentrated. Whenever I tried to remember those early years, the headaches came, the throbbing, the quivering nerves and the fear. Why should I be afraid? Why should I be gripped with apprehension even now? It did not make sense, and I considered myself a very sensible young woman.

I was eighteen years old. I had no illusions about myself. I realized that I would never be pretty with my pale face, blue-gray eyes and drab brown hair worn in tight braids on top of my head. I was plain, a dull, unremarkable girl with prim mannerisms, but I was intelligent, and I *was* sensible. Why, then, did my wrists feel weak, and why did I have this hollow sensation in the pit of my stomach? Why did Danver Hall represent a threat when it should represent a refuge? I could not understand it.

Danver Hall had been built over two hundred years ago by one of my ancestors. It had eventually passed into the hands of my father, as had the textile mill that provided the main means of livelihood for the citizens of Danmoor. I had been born in the house. Seven years later both my parents had been killed in a freak accident when part of the decayed west wing collapsed on them, and my uncle had inherited the house and the mill. He sent me away to school. The summons was the first direct communication I had had from him in eleven years.

The coach clattered over a particularly nasty rut, tossing me against the dusty cushions. The bag of mail tumbled to the floor with a dull thud, the contents rustling crisply. I smoothed the skirt of my dark blue dress and wiped a smudge of dust from my cheek, hoping my trunk fastened on top of the coach hadn't been knocked down. Sighing deeply, I made an effort to compose myself. It wouldn't do to arrive in Danmoor ruffled and disturbed. I must remain cool, in complete possession of myself.

I must accept facts.

My schooldays were over. I was entering upon a new phase of life, and I must adjust myself to whatever might come. I was penniless, an orphan. I had received my schooling only through the charity of my uncle. I had no recourse but to obey his will. The past eleven years were gone. I did not regret leaving the school with its dark brown walls and icy corridors, the lumpy dormitory beds and hard wooden chairs. I would not miss the tasteless food or the odors of dust and chalk and flushed bodies, nor would I miss the stern mistresses or the giggling girls who took such delight in teasing me. They never let me forget that I was an orphan, never let me forget my pale, plain face and the coronet of tight, ugly brown braids. I was dull Jane Danver, the bookworm, the prude, reading Virgil in the original while they chattered about ribbons and the delivery boys. I had been miserable, yes, but I had adjusted to the misery and there had been a certain security in it. Now that security was gone . . . I was cast adrift, heading for the unknown.

If only Jamintha could be with me.

She was my only friend. Opposites attract, they say, and Jamintha and I were as different as it would be possible for two young women to be, yet we had been close for eleven years. Whenever I was glum, whenever I was tired and depressed and suffering from one of the incessant headaches, Jamintha was there, a capricious sprite, her silvery laughter tinkling merrily, her irrepressible spirits putting me to shame and helping me forget my worries. I could depend on her. I could never have survived those long years without her. Would I ever see her again?

I thought about her promise that last night. I wondered if she would keep it.

I had been in my narrow room, staring at the shabby, brass bound trunk that took up most of the floor space. It was already packed, and I would be leaving first thing in the morning. The candle spluttered, casting wavering gold shadows on the damp brown wall. The other girls were asleep in their own rooms, but I was too upset, too excited to sleep. My head was throbbing, and I was dry-eyed, unable to shed the tears that would have provided some release. Shivering in my thin chemise, I watched the shadows dancing on the walls and listened to the silence that filled the dormitory. The candle flickered. There was a rustle of silken skirts. Jamintha crept into my room, a finger over her lips, her blue eyes filled with mischief. She stood by the trunk, listening, and then she laughed her merry, irreverent laugh.

"I had to come," she said. "I had to tell you good-bye. Oh Jane, are you really leaving this place?"

I nodded glumly.

"You're *lucky*," she replied. "*I* think it's ever so exciting. It'll be an adventure. Who knows what interesting things might happen? You may even meet a dashing young man and fall in *love*."

"There's not much chance of that," I said primly.

"Oh, Jane, you infuriate me, always belittling yourself. You've got ever so many nice features—you're pretty in fact. All you need is a little sparkle, a little vitality. If only you weren't so proper, so humorless—"

"I could never be like you," I said.

"But you *could* be," she insisted.

I shook my head, staring at her in the dim, flickering candlelight. Jamintha was everything I wasn't. She was everything I wanted to be. With her long, lustrous hair and sparkling blue eyes, she was undeniably beautiful. We were the same age, and both of us were orphans. We were the same size, too, and could wear the same dresses, but whereas Jamintha looked like a princess in her flowered silks, I looked like someone in drab masquerade. She radiated vitality and health, a bright, merry creature who found life a joyous adventure even in the dreary confines of the school. I had poor health, and I rarely smiled.

She whirled around, her silk skirt billowing over rustling petticoats. The dress was light blue, patterned with pink and lilac flowers. The bodice fit snugly over her full breasts and narrow waist. Rich chestnut curls fell to her shoulders, and her cheeks were flushed a delicate pink. I could see that she had some mischief in mind as she peered into the small, murky blue mirror that hung beside the door.

"It's terribly late," I said. "Why are you dressed? You should be in bed—"

"Pox on their silly rules and regulations," she retorted. "I'm going to see Billy. He's meeting me on the other side of the wall."

"You're slipping out again? If they should catch you—"

"To hell with them," Jamintha said sweetly. "They haven't caught me yet, have they? I'm very careful. Besides, Billy and I don't do anything *wicked*. He takes me to the music halls, and occasionally I let him steal a kiss. I'm quite as virginal as you are, Jane, although I'm not so *smug* about it."

"I wish you wouldn't use such language."

Jamintha smiled her pixie smile, delighted to have shocked me. I felt gauche and naive in her presence. Although she was only eighteen, although her life here at school had been as strict and closely supervised as my own had, Jamintha was surprisingly sophisticated. It was as though she had been born with a worldly knowledge I could never hope to possess. She was dazzling. I would pass unnoticed, but men would be unable to resist Jamintha. I felt no envy, just great admiration.

"I'll miss you," I said. "I don't know what I'll do without you, Jamintha."

"Just be glad you're leaving this dreadful school. If Charles Dickens were still alive he'd write an exposé of the place! Imagine living in such bleak, airless rooms and eating such incredible food—it's deplorable!"

"I'm afraid," I whispered.

"Nonsense!"

"I'll have no one to confide in. You're the only

friend I've ever had, the only one who—"

"I know," she interrupted, her lovely eyes serious. "We've been closer than sisters, Jane. It's meant as much to me as it has to you."

"What will become of you now?" I inquired. "You've graduated, too. Will you become a governess? Will you—"

"I haven't the slightest notion," she retorted. "I'll get by. I may even come to Danmoor."

"Why in the world would you do a thing like that?"

"To look after you, ninny. We need each other."

"If only you *could* come—"

Jamintha perched on the edge of the bed, lifting her skirts up to examine her pretty blue slippers. She avoided my eyes, but I could tell from her voice that she was as touched as I, as sad and disheartened.

"We're both alone," she said softly. "We've been through so much together. Dear Jane. You've made this place endurable these past years. I'll be lost without you."

"Jamintha—"

"I must go," she said, springing to her feet. "Billy will be waiting. He grows terribly impatient if I'm late. Goodbye, Jane. If you ever need me—*when* you need me—I'll be there. Somehow. I promise."

"Don't go," I protested. "There are so many things I want to—"

A gust of wind blew in through the corridor. The candle spluttered and almost went out, the tiny golden flame dancing wildly. There was a rustle of silk and the patter of light footsteps. Jamintha had vanished, and I was alone again, my headache worse than ever. The throbbing subsided after a while, and

I slept, my bones heavy with weariness. I grew so tired, so easily. If only I had Jamintha's blooming health. If only I weren't plagued with these headaches . . . I slept, dreading the morning and my departure.

The joggling coach brought me out of my reverie. I could hear the horse hooves pounding and the wheels rumbling. The springs creaked as though in agony, and it seemed the coach would surely fall apart as we hit another bump. The sky was a harsh steel color, the land beneath an expanse of sun-parched grass, boulders and bogs. How could people live in such a place? How could life exist in such depressing surroundings? The stunted trees lifted their gnarled limbs like arms raised in entreaty, a brisk wind already stripping them of their dark green leaves. It was a tormented landscape, a nightmare place fit only for the wind and the lashing rains.

Gradually, it changed. The rocky slopes became rolling hills, the sun-parched grass grew green, and I caught a glimpse of bright silver ribbon, a distant stream winding through the hills. The trees grew taller, powerful oaks spreading their heavy boughs and making cool purple shadows. Wildflowers grew, gold and yellow and brown, and I could see sheep grazing on a hillside. Danver County, I knew, was an oasis, a great patch of rich farmland completely surrounded by the moors. The village of Danmoor perched on the northeast edge, and the gardens of Danver Hall led directly into the moor where wild streams cascaded over mossy rocks and waterfalls poured into churning pools . . . How did I know that? Was I beginning to remember? I could see the rippling water, the boulders festooned with dark green moss, a bank of delicate purple wildflowers. Had I played there as a child? Would it all come back to me when I saw the house?

It grew late. The sun was beginning to make dark orange banners on the horizon. I began to see dwellings, scattered at first, then closer together. A farmer was plowing a loamy red-brown field, his forearms bronze in the dying sunlight. A group of children were romping around a barnyard and a dog joined in the play, barking loudly. The farms gave way to cottages, hovels, really, deplorable shacks with sagging roofs and narrow porches. These were where the mill-hands lived, trying to survive on miserable salaries. There was a clearing, and then I saw the mill itself sprawling over the land, long flat buildings without proper ventilation, smokestacks billowing gusts of ugly black smoke. Dark red flames glowed. I could see men pushing wheelbarrows through opened sheds, men sweating, men with embittered faces and stooped shoulders still at work even though the sun was almost gone.

The coach slowed as we came into the village. People sauntered aimlessly along the pavement. A group of old men perched on the benches around the square, staring at the tarnished bronze statue of Robert Danver, founder of Danmoor. There were shops and pubs, a hotel, a bank, brick walls stained with soot. The driver stopped in front of the tiny post office and got down to help me out. I stood on the pavement as he unstrapped my trunk and heaved it down, placing it beside me. He took the bag of mail out and disappeared into the post office, leaving me alone. There was no one to meet me.

Ten minutes passed, fifteen. The sun was gone

now, and the sky above sooty rooftops was deep blue streaked with purple. It was chilly, and I had no cloak. Where was my uncle? Today was September 12. Surely he remembered I was coming. I folded my arms about my waist, trying not to panic. Gusts of wind lifted my dark blue skirt, causing it to billow over the thin cotton petticoats. I was weary, so weary, and my head was aching again. Another migraine. Would I never be rid of them?

I stared around at the village of Danmoor: It was neat, even pretty with the arched rock bridges and the towering trees, but mill smoke had stained everything, and even though I stood in the middle of town I could sense the moors crouching just beyond, their desolation strongly felt. Through shadowy tree limbs at the end of town I could see a spire, a final ray of sunlight burnishing the copper. At least there was a church, I thought, though the village itself had a raw, rough hewn character. Life would be stern here, the men rugged, the women hard. There was none of the genteel charm usually associated with a small English village. I felt vulnerable and exposed, totally unprepared for this kind of atmosphere.

Across the street were three pubs in a row, noisy places with swinging wooden doors, bright yellow lights pouring through the windows making pools on the sidewalk. I could see dark figures moving around, and I heard loud, husky voices and raucous laughter. Someone was pounding on a piano, the music barely audible over the din. The coach driver stepped out of the post office with an empty bag. He climbed up on the seat and drove away to the livery stable. Still no one had come for me. I tried to still the trembling inside. The sky was dark now, and doorways and walls thronged with shadows as night approached.

I waited, growing more and more apprehensive.

The doors of the first pub across the street swung open and a tall man stepped out. He glanced at me without interest as the wind caused locks of unruly dark hair to tumble over his forehead. He was incredibly handsome with strong features and the build of an athlete. He wore highly polished black boots, tight gray breeches, a gray jacket that hung open to reveal an embroidered black satin waistcoat over his frilled white shirt. He had the arrogant demeanor of a cruel London rake and was as out of place here in Danmoor as I myself must be. He scowled, dark brows lowered, his wide mouth twisting with disgust. He was none too steady on his feet, weaving a little as he stood there, and I realized that he was drunk. He took a deep breath, chest swelling, and lifted a hand to brush his hair back from his forehead. I stared at him, fascinated and repelled at the same time.

A woman came out of the pub behind him. She had dark blonde hair, and there was a worried look in her eyes. The bodice of her vivid green dress was cut indecently low, a frilly white apron tied around her slender waist. Pretty in a coarse sort of way, she seemed on the verge of tears. She put her hand on the man's arm and looked up at him beseechingly.

"Come on back in, duckie," she pleaded. "You've 'ad a mite too much to drink. I'll fetch you some coffee and later—maybe later—"

"Leave me be," he retorted in a sullen voice.

"Don't be that way, luv. I—I'm sorry I pulled away from you. You were drunk, an' you lunged at me so suddenly—I didn't mean no harm. I'll let-ya come up to my room, duckie, sure I will, soon as you sober up. Let me give-ya some coffee—"

The man glared at her with dark eyes. The woman smiled nervously, obviously afraid of him. She was struggling to hold back the tears, and the man seemed to enjoy her plight. He smiled a cruel smile. Unworldly as I was I knew that such men considered women like the barmaid their personal chattels to be taken or discarded at will. His brooding good looks only made it worse. Women must spoil him deplorably, I thought, and he was well aware of the power he had over them.

"Please—" the barmaid said. "I'll lose my job, you see. If you walk out like this they'll sack me. You're our best customer an'—come on, luv. Be a sport—"

The man grinned a devilish grin. He raised his hand and examined it, turning it over to study the palm with great interest. Then he slammed it across her mouth with such force that she stumbled back against the wall. I could hear the impact of flesh on flesh from where I stood. The girl sank to her knees, sobbing. The man strolled on down the pavement and stepped into the next pub, leaving the wooden doors swinging behind him.

I was alarmed by what I had just seen and not a little frightened. I had listened to the girls chatter about sex. I had done extensive reading. I knew all the facts of life, but for eleven years I had been carefully sheltered against them. This incident which might have passed unnoticed by many seemed a raw, shocking display to me. Did men *really* treat women that way? The barmaid got to her feet and wiped away the tears and went back into the pub with a dejected air. I wondered who the man was. I wondered how anyone could be so thoroughly hateful. Not all men were like that, surely, but then not all men were so wickedly handsome.

An empty farm wagon came rolling down the street, the driver a husky lad who held the reins loosely in his lap. The dappled gray horse plodded at a lazy pace, the wagon creaking. Seeing me standing alone beside the shabby trunk, the driver pulled up on the reins and the wagon stopped a few yards away. The lad stared at me in surprise, and I took a step backward, my heart pounding. I was alone on a dark street. The boy was large, powerfully built. His mouth spread in a wide grin. He wore muddy brown boots, clinging tan trousers and a leather jerkin over a coarse white linen shirt. Thick, shaggy blond hair spilled over his forehead. His blue eyes stared at me openly.

"No one come to pick you up?" he inquired.

"Go away," I replied coldly.

"It's gettin' late," he remarked. "Looks like you need to hitch a ride with someone."

"Go away," I repeated, my voice beginning to tremble.

He grinned again. It was a surprisingly amiable grin. The lad couldn't have been much older than I, and he had a rough, affable manner that was almost pleasant, despite the circumstances. Undeniably raw-boned and crude, he was nevertheless attractive. His grin was appealing, and those vivid blue eyes were full of mischief.

"'Ey now," he said, "you're not afraid-a me, are you?"

"Not in the least," I lied. "Just go away."

"You plannin' to walk to Danver 'all?"

"How do you know—"

"You're Miss Jane Danver, aren't-ja? Susie told me they were expectin' you. Looks like someone forgot to come fetch you."

"Susie?"

"She works there at Danver 'all, the maid. We're courtin'. Soon as I get enough ready cash in my pockets I'm aimin' to marry 'er, though the wench 'asn't said yes yet. You want I should drive you to the 'all? I 'aven't got anything better to do."

"I—I think not."

He chuckled. It was a rich, jovial sound.

"I'm Johnny Stone, Ma'am. I'm hell with the lasses, all right, as Susie'll tell-ya. Nothin' I like so much as a good tumble, but I ain't never taken it by force, an' I got respect for my betters. I'm just tryin' to be 'elpful, ma'am. I ain't plannin' rape. You'd best let me drive you to Danver 'all."

"I—"

"It's a long walk, an' it isn't safe for you to be alone like this. A lotta fellows, now, they 'aven't got my scruples."

He swung down from the seat and picked up the heavy trunk as though it were a feather, swinging it into the back of the wagon. He was tall, six foot four at least, with enormous shoulders and lean waist. I was still a bit frightened, but he smiled reassuringly, exuding a friendly warmth that caused my fears to vanish.

"I—I don't know why there was no one to meet me," I said. "My uncle knew I was supposed to arrive on the mail coach."

"There ain't no tellin'," Johnny replied. "The

folks who live up there in the big 'ouse—they're a peculiar lot, an' that's for sure."

"What do you mean?"

"I reckon you'll be finding out for yourself," he said tersely.

Without warning, he wrapped his large hands around my waist and swung me up onto the seat in one swift motion. I gave a little cry of alarm as my skirts billowed, revealing stockinged calves. Johnny chuckled, amused, then climbed heavily onto the seat beside me, gathering up the reins. He smelled of sweat and the barnyard, a pungent aroma that was not at all unpleasant. It seemed to suit him. He clicked the reins and the wagon began to rattle down the street, the dappled-gray as slow and lazy as before.

"I remember you," Johnny said casually.

"You do?"

"From before, when you was a little girl. You were a pretty thing, I don't mind sayin', always laughing and carryin' on like a regular princess. You wore frilly dresses, an' you were always gettin' into scrapes, runnin' wild so to speak."

"I—I can't recall any of that."

"Sure, you were a regular menace, but everyone adored-ja. Things were different then. The village was a 'appy place. Your father—'e 'ad respect for the men workin' at the mill, treated 'em squarely. I was nine years old when the accident 'appened at the big 'ouse. The whole village grieved for your folks."

"The village has changed?"

"Aye, an' that's the truth. Your uncle—well, it ain't my place to be speakin' against your kin. I'll just say that I'm glad I'm not under 'is thumb. I got my own farm—my folks left it to me when they died. It ain't much, granted, but at least I don't hafta sweat blood at the mill like most men in this town."

"You're saying my uncle is unjust?"

"I'm sayin' 'e's a bloody tyrant. 'E owns the mill, an' most of the town, too. 'E 'as a stranglehold on the men, an' 'e squeezes without mercy, chokin' the breath out of 'em. The mill produces some of the finest fabrics in all England, aye, but at what a cost." His voice was quiet and lazy, giving his words an even greater impact.

"You don't like my uncle?"

"I won't lie to you, Ma'am. I don't, an' that's for sure. I ain't afraid of 'im, though, like most folks around these parts."

"People fear him?"

"An' for good reason. Someone displeases 'im an' they lose their job. That leaves 'em two alternatives: look for work outside-a Danver County or starve to death. No one 'ud 'ire a man your uncle dismissed. No one 'ud dare."

Johnny shook his head, frowning. The wagon passed down a quiet street with small, neat houses set back behind carefully clipped lawns, oak trees making a rustling leafy canopy above. Lights burned in windows, warm yellow squares against the darkness, and there were pleasant sounds and an atmosphere of comfort. The merchants and shopkeepers lived here, I assumed. It was quite different from the shacks of the millhands and their families. I wondered if what Johnny had said about my uncle was really true. Was he a tyrant? Did he rule his domain with an iron will, punishing any who dared to defy him? This was Victorian England, not the Middle Ages, yet there were still grave abuses of power. Perhaps the boy exaggerates, I told myself, disconcerted by his words.

The wagon rumbled over a rustic stone bridge that arched across the river. There was a rushing sound and the scent of moss and mud, and the water gleamed silver blue under the first rays of moonlight. We were soon on the outskirts of Danmoor. The sky was the color of ashes, and the moon was thin and pale. I could smell the strong, peaty smell of the moors.

"How far is it to Danver Hall?" I inquired.

"A couple of miles," he said, surprised. "Don't-ja remember?"

I shook my head. "I don't remember anything about the house. I don't remember anything about my uncle. It's as though—as though my life began on my first day at school."

"Yeah? You mean you don't even remember your folks?"

"I have no memories of them whatsoever."

Johnny made no comment. I thought he was being tactful.

"I—I suppose that seems peculiar to you," I remarked.

"'Course not," he said. "You was just a tot when they sent you away. You were at the 'ouse the night the accident 'appened. It must-a been awful for you. I reckon you just closed it all out. Things like that 'appen, I 'ear."

"Perhaps you're right."

"Reckon it ain't meant for you to remember," he said philosophically. "I wouldn't worry none about it, Ma'am. Yesterday is gone, and we 'ave-ta think about today and make plans for tomorrow."

Johnny clicked the reins and fell silent. He was a very sympathetic young man, amiable, relaxed, easy to talk to. I sensed compassion and understanding, or else I would not have told him so much. With his large, ponderous body and casual, confident manner, he emanated masculinity and strength, a highly physical man who could nevertheless be gentle. The maid Susie could consider herself fortunate to have such a man to take care of her. Young Johnny was a prize. I hoped she appreciated him.

"Does my uncle live alone at Danver Hall?" I asked.

"Hunh? Seems so strange your not knowing. No, there's the son. He'd be your cousin. Master Brence Danver, a 'ellion if there ever was one."

"Why do you say that?"

"Ask anyone around these parts. A demon, 'e is, 'andsome as Satan before the Fall an' twice as mean. Drinkin' and wenchin'—them's 'is occupations. An brawlin', too. Always gettin' into fights an' usually winnin'. 'E's a bad 'un. I ain't talkin' outta turn, Ma'am, ain't tellin' you nothin' you won't find out for yourself soon's you meet 'im."

"What about my aunt?"

"I hear tell she died from some kind-a influenza when Brence was just a toddler. Charles Danver was a widower when 'e came to take over Danver 'all. Brence was fifteen at the time. I reckon 'e's twenty-six now, seein' as 'ow eleven years 'as passed. Danver never re-married, though there's that French woman—" He cut himself short, obviously afraid he had gone too far.

"French woman?" I prompted.

"Madame DuBois," Johnny replied, pronouncing it "Dew-Boy." "She's the 'ousekeeper, 'as been for all these years. There's some as say she's somethin' more, Susie included. Skinny woman, looks like a painted maypole with her make-up and ribbons. She doesn't like *me*, I can tell you for sure, but then I don't reckon she likes anyone who ain't gentry."

So my uncle has a housekeeper, I thought. I knew exactly what Johnny was implying. I should have been shocked, but I wasn't. The rigid proprieties taught in a girls' school did not extend to society at large. I was rapidly finding that out.

"It isn't a 'appy place, Danver 'all. Some say it's cursed. Some say it's 'aunted. That's nonsense, a-course, but I can see as 'ow some folks'd believe it. Susie's always talkin' about strange noises, and I've seen the lights myself."

"The—lights?"

"In the west wing. It's all in ruins, the walls collapsed, the ceilin' fallen through in places. Mysterious lights flicker there, always late at night. Gives folks the shivers, though I reckon there's an explanation for 'em."

I made no reply, but thought about all I had learned these past few minutes. We were passing through a wooded area now, dark tree limbs reaching out on either side, fireflies creating luminous golden lights that floated among the dense shrubs. The horse's hooves clattered on the hard dirt road. The wagon made squeaky, groaning noises. Johnny sensed my apprehension. He turned to me, and when he spoke his husky voice was gentle.

"I didn't mean to alarm you, Miss Jane. I shouldn't-a told you them things, but seein' as 'ow you didn't know what to expect—"

"Thank you, Johnny. I appreciate what you've told me."

We left the woods behind. The pungent odor of peat was stronger than ever, and I could hear the wind sweeping over the moors, an anguished sound full of desolation. Moonlight streamed down, creating a world of black and gray and tarnished silver, shadows moving as wispy clouds floated over the surface of the moon. I leaned forward, peering at the horizon. Danver Hall loomed like some monstrous folly created by a madman.

CHAPTER TWO

At one time it must have been majestic, but the years had taken their toll. The west wing was a shambles, a labyrinth of partially standing walls and heaps of huge gray stones, all bathed in moonlight and silhouetted against the night sky. The central portion was intact, a small tower at either end of the portico, and the east wing was solid. Built of stone, the multi-level roofs a soot-stained green, Danver Hall had no beauty, nothing to alleviate the gloom. It must look even worse in sunlight, I thought, as the wagon drew nearer. Beyond the west wing, across a stretch of shabby gardens and some distance from the house itself, stood the Dower House, a small, compact house made of the same materials, sheltered by the enormous oak trees that grew all over the property.

"Not much to look at, is it?" Johnny said, clicking the reins and urging the horse to a faster pace.

"It's not—too attractive," I agreed.

"They don't build 'ouses like that anymore, and thank the Lord. Impossible to 'eat, impossible to keep clean. It's too bulky, too 'eavy. The west wing 'as already crumbled, an' one of these days the rest of it's goin' to topple over and sink into the bog."

"The Dower House looks sturdy enough," I remarked.

"Ah, there's a sore spot. The 'ouse and the acres around it were sold over a 'undred years ago, passed out of the family 'ands. Dower 'ouse belongs to some gentleman in London. 'E rents it out ever now 'n then. The Danvers don't take to the idea, an' that's a fact, but there isn't anything they can do about it."

"Who would want to rent it?" I mused.

"Not many, I can assure-ya. No one's lived there for ten years, but it's been kept up. Well, Miss Jane, 'ere we are—"

The wagon passed through two tall stone portals, a heavy wrought-iron gate standing open, and proceeded along the crushed shell drive that circled in front of the portico. Johnny stopped the wagon, leaped down and reached for my hand. He held it in a firm grip as I stepped down. We stood on the steps that led up to the portico spanning the length of the central portion of the house. No lamps burned, and the moonlight only emphasized the darkness. Crickets rasped between cracks in the stone, and there was the constant, mournful sound of the wind.

I trembled inside, the panic starting to rise, and Johnny held on to my hand, squeezing it tightly.

"There now," he said huskily, "it'll be all right. Susie'll look after you. She's eager to 'ave someone 'er own age about. Don't worry, Miss Jane."

"I wish I weren't such a coward."

"'Ell, you're just a lass, an' anyone'd be upset seein' this place for the first time. You buck up, 'ear? People in the village remember you, an' they're 'appy to 'ave you back."

His words made me feel better. I managed to compose myself as he took the trunk out of the wagon and carried it under the portico, setting it beside the immense black oak door. Reaching for the heavy brass knocker, he pounded it against the solid wood. I could hear the noise echoing within, and in a moment there was the sound of footsteps ringing on a marble floor. Through the panes of the side windows I could see a light flickering wildly as someone approached.

The door swung open. A girl with long tarnished gold curls and saucy brown eyes peered up at Johnny, the lamp held aloft in her hand. She took a step backward, her small pink lips parting in surprise.

"What are *you* doing here?" she exclaimed. "If Madame DuBois sees you about the place—of all the cheek! Knocking on the front door to boot! I think you've taken leave of your senses, Johnny Stone! That's the only explanation!"

"None-a your sass, girl," he said in a stern voice.

"Leave at once before she hears us, you hulking oaf!"

"You'd best watch your tongue, Missy," he warned.

"Johnny," she whispered, truly alarmed. "Whatever possessed you—"

"I've brung Miss Jane," he retorted. "There weren't no one to meet 'er an' she was standin' all by 'erself right across the street from the pubs. I reckoned I'd best pick 'er up before somethin' unpleasant 'appened."

"Miss Jane?" the girl said, standing on tiptoe to

peer over his broad shoulder. "Master Brence was supposed to fetch her. He hasn't returned, and we assumed—"

Johnny stepped aside, and the girl saw me for the first time. About my height, she had a slender waist, and the bodice of her snug pink dress emphasized a well-developed figure. Tarnished gold curls tumbled to her shoulders in rich profusion. Pert, full of vitality, Susie had a hoydenish charm I found immediately winning. Setting the lamp down on a table, she gave Johnny a push and stepped outside to greet me, her lively brown eyes full of genuine warmth.

"I've been looking forward to this," she said. "We all have. I can't imagine why Master Brence wasn't there—I can, too, but never mind. Come on inside—" She led me into an enormous hall with black and white marble floor. The lower half of the walls were paneled in dark mahogany, with purple and blue wallpaper above. Doors led off in different directions, and at one side a spiral staircase with mahogany banisters curled up to the second floor. The lamp provided little light, casting long shadows around the room.

Johnny stood lingering in the doorway. Susie shot him an exasperated look. "Don't just stand there, you clumsy lout! Pick up her trunk and bring it in."

Johnny lowered his brows menacingly, but he did as she said. Heaving the trunk up and stepping inside, he kicked the door shut with his foot. It slammed with a loud bang.

"Now you've done it!" Susie cried.

There was a sound of someone approaching through the shadows, and then the gaslights in sconces about the room flickered, blossoming into dim yellow radiance. The woman who had turned them on came toward us. Susie had a worried expression. Johnny stood with the trunk balanced on one shoulder, a sheepish grin on his lips, looking for all the world like an overgrown boy caught with his hand in a cookie jar. Still uneasy, my nerves on edge, I stared at the bizarre figure of Helene DuBois.

She was almost six foot tall and extremely thin. Her black hair was streaked with silver and worn in an elaborate coiffure. With her incredible make-up she did indeed resemble a painted maypole, her face long, the dark eyes haughty, the thin lips a bright red. She wore a dress of deep purple taffeta, a ring of heavy bronze keys dangling from the belt. There was a sour, pinched look about her, and when she spoke her voice was like chipped ice.

"What is going on, Susie?" she asked, ignoring me.

"Miss Jane has arrived. Master Brence wasn't there to fetch her. Johnny happened by in his wagon. He brought her to the house."

"I see," the housekeeper said.

She turned to Johnny, her eyes full of loathing. He might have been some bloodthirsty criminal come to steal the silver. "Since you are here, you may as well take the trunk up to her room," she said crisply.

"I reckon I might," he said in a lazy drawl.

"I'm certain Susie will be delighted to show you the way."

"Come on, Johnny," Susie said.

She walked toward the staircase, and Johnny sauntered after her, the trunk on his shoulder. Helene DuBois looked at me for the first time. Her thin lips moved in an unconvincing smile, but her eyes remained flat. She examined me for a moment without saying anything, openly disdainful of what she saw. This woman did not like me. She did not want me here. I had no idea why, but there could be no mistake about the barely concealed animosity.

"I'm sorry if you've been inconvenienced," she remarked. "Brence must have missed the mail coach."

"There was no inconvenience. Johnny was quite kind."

Her thin nostrils flared. "A most undesirable specimen. I endeavored to employ him to keep the stables clean, and he had the audacity to refuse. It's just as well, I suppose, with Susie around. She's no better than she should be, either, but then it's impossible to find decent servants nowadays."

"Indeed?" I said coolly.

"We have only three. Susie, of course, and Cook, and the gardener, but he just comes twice a week."

"And yourself," I added, unable to restrain myself.

Her expression did not alter, but I could see that I had struck home. Her heavy eyelids narrowed ever so slightly. She was trying to decide if my comment had been a deliberate insult.

"You *are* my uncle's housekeeper, are you not?"

"That is correct," she answered stiffly.

"Then would you kindly inform him that I have arrived."

"He has retired for the night. He will see you in the morning. Susie will be down in a few moments and will show you to your room. Is there anything you require in the meantime?"

"No, thank you. The driver stopped at an inn along the way, and I had a quite sufficient meal."

She had not mentioned feeding me. My words were a veiled reprimand of her thoughtlessness. She sensed it.

"Very good," she replied.

She stared at me for a few seconds more, the dark eyes flat, and then she left, her stiff taffeta skirt rustling. I had made an enemy of the woman, but I really didn't care. For all my timidity, I had a dreadful temper and could be as sharp-tongued and acid as the best of them. Her comments about Johnny and the maid had infuriated me, and I couldn't help resist putting Madame DuBois in her place. I might be sorry for it later on, but at the moment I was pleased to have scored a point.

Footsteps sounded on the stairs. Susie came down, rubbing her backside and looking peeved. Johnny was right behind her, his grin wider than ever. Susie dismissed him in imperious tones and informed him that he needn't expect to see her on her next afternoon off as she wanted nothing more to do with such an uncivilized and *grabby* individual.

"I reckon you'll be comin' 'round, all right," he said lazily. "I'll be waitin', luv."

"Off with you!" she snapped impatiently, holding the door open.

Johnny shambled outside, chuckling to himself. Susie closed the door firmly and tossed her head, dark golden curls bouncing.

"I guess I showed *him*," she said. "Just because he has the most maddening blue eyes, he thinks he can take any liberty he's a-mind to. I told him off proper, I did. Isn't he glorious, Miss Jane? Have you ever *seen* such shoulders?"

"Johnny is a very pleasant lad," I agreed.

"He's a prize, all right, though I wouldn't tell *him* that. He's conceited enough as it is! Those village hussies flock around him something awful, and he just stands there with a grin, soaking it all in. I have to keep my eye on him *con*stantly!"

Susie pushed the curtain aside from one of the windows and peeked out, watching her lover drive away in his creaking wagon. After a moment she let the curtain fall back in place and turned around, smiling a pensive smile. There was a rapturous look in her eyes as she thought secret thoughts.

"Madame has gone, I see," she said, coming back down to earth. "She loathes Johnny. He came to call on me one day and she told him to go sweep out the stables! He told *her* he owned his own farm and she could bloody well do it herself. She almost fainted!"

"She has forbidden you to see him?"

"She would if she could," Susie replied airily, "but she doesn't dare. I'd quit, and she'd never be able to replace me. I'm a treasure, you see, and what's more, no one from the village will work here. They're afraid of Charles Danver and Son."

"You're not from the village?"

"Do I *look* like a country bumpkin?" she asked, offended. "No, indeed. I was born and raised on Whitechapel Road. Cook and I both are from London. Mister Charles brought us here three years ago—I was fifteen at the time. The gardener is a local man, but he only comes twice a week and never steps foot inside the house. I imagine you're weary, Miss Jane," she continued, changing the subject. "You must be eager to see your room."

Susie chattered blithely as we climbed the curving stairs. She led the way down a long, wide hall, through a shorter one and then down a flight of narrow stairs that brought us to the ground floor again. I found it impossible to get my bearings. Gas lights burned in sconces here and there along the way, but they did little to alleviate the gloom. This section of the house was even colder than the front hall, and there was an icy draft, as though several windows had been left open.

"Aren't we moving toward the west wing?" I inquired, not trusting my sense of direction.

Susie nodded. "Mister Charles and Master Brence live in the east wing, and Madame felt you'd be better satisfied on this side of the house. Master Brence frequently comes in late, you see, and—well, *noisy*. You won't be disturbed over here."

"I see."

"Your room's ever so cozy. When I learned you were coming, I fixed it up myself."

The draft grew stronger and stronger. Both our skirts were fluttering now, and the gas lights were wavering beneath their globes, casting frenzied shadows across the wall. The hall was intersected by another one leading directly into the west wing. As we passed it, I could see the ruined walls, the fallen stones and patches of moonlit sky where the ceilings had caved in. Susie paused for a moment, and we stared at the ruined wing. The wind eddied around the broken walls and jumbled heaps of stone, whistling loudly, raising clouds of dust. Susie's hair flew about her face, and she reached for my hand, squeezing it.

"Why—why haven't they closed it off?" I said, my voice barely audible over the soaring wind.

Susie shook her head, indicating that she had no idea.

Standing there in the wind, I thought of what had happened eleven years ago. My mother, my father—strangers whose faces I couldn't remember—had been buried beneath that rubble. There had been an explosion . . . In the back of my mind I could hear the noise, the low rumble, the crash as stones began to fall. I shivered, holding Susie's hand tightly.

As we moved on down the hall, the gusts of cold air were not as fierce as before. There was an abrupt turn, and the narrow back hall began, leading back toward the east. Susie opened the door of a corner room and led me inside.

"My own room's just a short way down the back hall," she said, "near the servants' stairs. We're rather isolated, but I think you'll be glad. You—you won't be *scared*, will you?"

"Of course not," I said primly.

"I'm not. There are noises—footsteps, like someone prowling among the rubble—but I have enough sense to know it's only the wind. Folks say the west wing's haunted and the ghosts prowl at night, but that's a lot of foolishness."

"I'm sure it is," I replied.

My room was small and pleasant. A fire burned cozily in the marble fireplace, lusty orange flames devouring the charred logs, and lamps glowed. A tattered Aubusson carpet covered the floor, the pink and lilac patterns faded, and the wainscotting had been painted white, a light blue paper above. A blue and lilac canopy draped over the enormous four poster, and there was a small desk and an immense wardrobe. All three had been recently painted white. There was even an overstuffed chair of nap-worn velvet with a lamp hanging from the ceiling beside it with a blue and red stained glass shade. A big mirror in ornate, tarnished gold frame tilted over an elegant white dresser, and one long, wide window faced the back of the house, billowing sky blue curtains hanging before it.

"It was terribly gloomy before," Susie admitted. "Everything was dark and solemn. I used lots of white paint—took me days to do it—and sewed the canopy and curtains myself. I'm very handy with a needle."

"That was very thoughtful of you. Susie. The room is charming."

"I pictured the kind of room *I* would like to have and then set to work. Madame was all too happy to turn it over to me. *She* certainly didn't intend to put herself out to make things pleasant."

"I—had the impression she didn't like me," I said hesitantly, fully aware that I shouldn't be discussing it with the maid.

"Oh, she doesn't like anyone," Susie said flippantly. "Besides Mister Charles, that is. She likes *him* all right. She has her own apartment in the east wing. Mighty convenient, if you know what I mean."

I did, but I made no comment.

"She doesn't even get along with Master Brence, but then that's understandable. I avoid him myself. He pulled me into the pantry just once—I was barely sixteen—and he was mighty surprised at the reception he got. There was a terrible bruise on his shin, and he hobbled around with a limp for a week afterward. I could'uv been sacked, of course, but he didn't tell his father about it. He's never bothered me since, either."

I knelt to loosen the straps of my trunk, not really surprised by what she had told me. Brence Danver was obviously a blighter, and pretty housemaids were the natural prey of such men, though Susie, it seemed, was perfectly capable of fending for herself. Master Brence would present no problem as far as I was concerned. Men don't clutch at pale, plain young women with prim mannerisms and coronets of tight braids. My cousin would probably find it hard even to be civil.

Susie helped me unpack. Together we took out my simple, rather drab dresses. All were in shades of gray and blue, tan and brown, only one or two even halfway attractive. Susie was disappointed, expecting to see a grand wardrobe. She hung the dresses in the large wardrobe, and we took out the petticoats and plain white cotton underclothes. There were no silk stockings, no velvet furbelows, no fancy patent leather shoes. My clothes were like me, plain and unexciting.

"Have you no party dresses?" Susie asked as we finished.

"There were no occasions to wear them at school," I said.

"Surely you had holidays—"

"I spent my holidays at school."

"That's sad," Susie said quietly. "You haven't had much fun, have you, Miss Jane?"

"My uncle enabled me to receive a fine education," I replied. "I speak French fluently and read Latin. I'm familiar with all the classics, and I am an authority on eighteenth-century French history."

"Fiddlesticks!" she retorted, completely unimpressed. "That'll never help you get a fellow."

"I'm not interested in beaux," I said, beginning to find the girl's familiarity a bit trying.

JAMINTHA

"Sure you are," Susie persisted. "Every girl is. Didn't you meet any fellows at that school?"

"We were kept under strict supervision."

"Ha! That wouldn't-a stopped *me*."

It hadn't stopped Jamintha either, I thought, remembering the escapades she had described with such delight. How many times had she slipped over the wall? How many times had she crept into my room, dreamy-eyed and smiling a weary smile? Had I secretly envied her? Had I wished I had the spirit to live with boldness and dash? Of course not, I told myself, arranging the dresses on their hangers and closing the wardrobe door. I was too cool and rational not to see the folly of such conduct.

"You *could* get a beau if you wanted one, Miss Jane," Susie said quietly. "You have very nice features."

"I'm sure you mean well, Susie, but I have no illusions about myself. Mirrors don't lie."

My voice was stiff and formal, discouraging any further comments, but Susie was undeterred.

"Those braids are far too severe," she remarked. "Your hair should fall in loose, natural waves, framing your face. I could do wonders with you. A new hairstyle, a bit of powder, a spot of rouge—"

"That will be quite enough, Susie," I said sharply. "What are we to do with this trunk?"

"There's an empty wardrobe down the hall. I sometimes keep my mops and dust rags there. It's more than big enough to hold the trunk."

Empty now, the trunk was still heavy, and Susie found it difficult to lift. I went over to help her, dropping my formal manner. The girl was a lively, amiable creature, naturally enthusiastic. She had meant no harm. I was sorry I had been so harsh.

Together we carried the trunk a few yards down the back hall to where the old mahogany wardrobe stood. The varnish was peeling, and the piece was so large that it almost blocked the passage. Susie tugged on the knob, trying to open it, but moisture had caused the wood to swell and the door was stuck. It was only after several minutes of frantic pulling that it finally swung open, creaking on its hinges. We stored the trunk inside, closed the heavy door and returned to my room.

"Is there anything else I can do for you?" Susie inquired.

"Everything seems to be in order," I replied.

"The backstairs lead directly down into the kitchen," she told me. "Cook never locks anything up. Perhaps I could fetch you a snack, a glass of milk, maybe—"

"No, thank you, Susie. When is breakfast served?"

"No one ever has breakfast together," she told me. "Cook and I arrange trays and carry them in. I'll bring yours when I wake you up."

"That will be fine."

"Welcome to Danver Hall, Miss Jane," she said.

The girl executed a clumsy curtsy and left the room, pulling the door shut behind her. I had been eager to be rid of her, but now that she was gone the room seemed curiously forlorn. I stood quietly for a few minutes, trying to master my emotions. I was alone at last, and that was when the sadness came, when the panic seemed to well up and threaten to overcome me. I knew I couldn't give way to it. I knew I had to cope, but it was going to be extremely difficult.

JAMINTHA

Self pity is for fools, Jane, I admonished myself. You are eighteen years old, a grown woman. *Act* like a grown woman.

I briskly began to prepare for bed, forcing myself to put all disturbing thoughts aside. Removing my dress and petticoats, I hung them in the wardrobe and, wearing only a thin cotton chemise, sat down at the dresser to unbraid my hair. I brushed it vigorously, staring into the mirror with level blue-gray eyes. A black ormolu clock ticked on the mantle. The fire had burned down, the log a heap of crackling pink-gold ashes. I turned off the lamps and climbed into bed.

The coarse white linen sheets were crisp, smelling of soap, and the heavy violet satin comforter was deliciously warm. I was incredibly weary, but sleep evaded me. Through the openings of the canopy I watched shadows frolic over the walls like dark black demons, alternating with flecks of moonlight. Night noises abounded, floorboards groaning, joints settling, underlined by the anguished sound of the wind sweeping over the moor. Someone was prowling in the west wing. I could hear footsteps stumbling over the loose stones. No . . . it was the wind, only the wind. Eventually my eyelids grew heavy and welcome oblivion came.

I awoke abruptly from a sound sleep. In the moonlight the hands of the clock showed three o'clock in the morning. The noise had been loud, jerking me into consciousness. I sat up, completely awake, every nerve taut. Someone was laughing, a rich, uproarious laughter that rang clear in the night. The sound seemed to be coming from outside. My heart pounding, I slipped out of bed and moved to the window, brushing the curtain aside to peer out through the misty pane.

The gardens were bathed in moonlight, shrubs casting long shadows. I could see the carriage house and stables to one side and, behind the line of trees, the moors beyond. Someone was moving along the flagstone path. He was moving quite unsteadily, head lowered, hands thrust into the pockets of his trousers. He stumbled near the lily pond, almost tumbling into the water. Emitting a loud curse, he stared at the house, the wind tearing at his hair and causing his jacket to flap. It was too dark and he was too far away for me to discern any features, but I could tell that my cousin Brence was tall with a lean, powerful build. After a moment he staggered on toward the house, moving out of my line of vision. What demon drove him? What made him stay out till all hours, indulging in such deplorable vices? I went back to bed, disturbed at what I had seen.

I finally slept. I dreamed of Jamintha. I dreamed she was sitting on the edge of the bed. She spoke to me in a comforting voice. She told me not to worry. She promised to come as soon as possible.

CHAPTER THREE

Charles Danver was waiting to see me. Susie had knocked on the door to inform me of this fact. Before returning to her duties she had told me how to locate the drawing room, her directions simple and clear. He was waiting, and still I had not left my room. It was after ten o'clock. I had had my breakfast two hours ago. It was raining outside, sheets of swirling rain pouring over the countryside, creating a wet, muddy, desolate world. It pounded noisily on the roof and it made glistening silver-brown webs over the window panes. There was no sunlight, and the room was so dim that I could barely see my reflection in the large mirror over the dressing table.

I was nervous. I wanted him to like me. I wanted him to approve of me. I wanted to be pretty and vivacious like Jamintha, the kind of niece a man like Charles Danver could appreciate. I had selected my dress with care. It was my best, sprigged muslin, tiny blue and violet flowers against a gray backgound. I had braided my hair into a tight, neat coronet on top of my head, but the effect was still dismal. There were shadows about my eyes, and my face was too pale, the skin stretched tightly over high cheekbones, the nicely shaped lips only faintly pink. If only I had Jamintha's luxuriant coloring. If only my blue-gray eyes could sparkle as hers did. Jamintha would have greeted my uncle with teasing aplomb. I could only try to still the nervous tremors inside.

I finally left the room, following Susie's directions. I tried to remember the house. I must have known it well as a child. I must have been familiar with every room. Had I raced down these long halls, sliding on the highly polished wooden floors? Had I hidden behind those dusty red velvet curtains, investigated those dark corners and recessed stairs? The house was completely unfamiliar. I might never have been here before. I moved quietly across the main hall and followed the narrow passageway that led to the drawing room. The great mahogany doors were closed. I paused in front of them, trying to summon enough courage to knock.

My knuckles rapped gently against the polished wood. A stern masculine voice commanded me to enter.

The room was enormous, the lower section of the walls paneled in rich brown walnut, the paper above a light green with swirls of darker green and dull gold. Faded oriental rugs covered sections of the dark parquet floor, and although the furniture was heavy and oppressive the room was so immense that it seemed sparsely furnished. A long green velvet sofa crouched before the huge marble fireplace. A fire burned behind the brass screen, tall black andirons holding stout, crackling logs, yet the room remained icy cold. A row of French windows, tightly closed now, opened out into the northeast gardens. The stiff green brocade draperies had been left opened, and through the dripping panes I could see part of the stables beyond.

No lamps burned. The room was dim. My uncle was standing in the shadows. I did not see him at first.

"Uncle Charles?" I said.

He moved away from the huge sideboard where he had been pouring brandy from a tarnished silver decanter. Glass in hand, he approached, pausing a few yards away from me to take a swallow. He did not speak. He stood there drinking his brandy and staring at me with the cool objectivity a scientist might give to a curious new specimen. His dark eyes took in every detail, yet they showed no reaction. His manner was intolerably rude, but it gave me an opportunity to study him in turn.

Charles Danver was forty-five years old. He was a large man, solidly built, with broad shoulders and a strong lean body that had begun to thicken just slightly with middle age. His black boots were highly glossed, his dark broadcloth suit expertly tailored to minimize the excess weight. The plum colored vest was embroidered with black silk, and a buff colored stock rested against his chin. He was still impressively handsome with unruly raven black hair and strong, virile features. Thick black brows arched over the stern, dark brown eyes, and the lids were heavy, giving him a lazy, insolent look. The nose was large, slightly crooked, and the wide mouth was undeniably sensual.

Men would be intimidated by my uncle, and certain women would find him irresistible. Hard, unscrupulous, fully aware of his power, he would seize what he wanted without the least regard to others. He would take a cruel satisfaction in crushing an enemy, and he would treat his women with a cold, arrogant disdain. I sensed this instinctively, and I knew that everything Johnny had told me about him was true.

"Your hands are shaking," he said.

"I—I'm sorry," I replied, clasping them together.

"You find me frightening?"

I nodded, unable to speak.

His lips curled into a sarcastic smile. He finished his glass of brandy and set it on a table, his eyes never leaving my face. His complexion was ruddy. The flesh was beginning to sag at the jaw, and there was the faint suggestion of a double chin. Strangely enough, this only made him all the more attractive, and Charles Danver was a vastly attractive man. He had authority, a commanding presence that would put many younger men to shame.

"Many people find me intimidating," he admitted.

And you revel in it, I thought, standing there with my hands clasped tightly at my waist.

"So you are Jane," he said in a bored, lazy voice. "I must apologize for my son's failure to meet you. He left the house early and, unfortunately, stepped into one of the pubs. He spent the night drinking and whoring, completely forgetting his reason for going to the village."

I tried not to look shocked, but Charles Danver noticed.

"Do I startle you? I see no reason to mince words about my son. He is a profligate young scoundrel, pickling his brain with alcohol, squandering his energy on women—and with his name and devilish good looks they're all too available. When he was younger I could beat him into submission, but he's too old to thrash now. The only hold I have over him is a financial one. I control the purse strings, and therefore I have at least some control over my son. Not much, I grant you, but enough to keep him from completely kicking over the traces."

I made no comment. From what I had seen last night, I imagined that Master Brence Danver was enough to turn even the kindliest father into a stern patriarch. He was no doubt in his room this very moment, sleeping off the effects of last night's dissipations. I wondered how long it would be before I met my cousin. It was not a meeting I looked forward to with anticipation.

"You're not a pretty girl, Jane," my uncle said abruptly.

"No, Sir," I replied with lowered lashes.

"Speak up, girl, and look at me when you speak."

I raised my eyes. Charles Danver was smiling. He was enjoying this. He was a natural bully, and he gloried in his ability to intimidate me. I tried to look at him with a level gaze. He opened a porcelain box and took out a slender brown cigar, lighting it and narrowing his eyes to avoid the smoke.

"You have none of your mother's beauty, none of her vitality."

"She was—beautiful?" I asked.

He nodded, a crease between his brows. He looked almost angry.

"And my father?" I inquired.

"I have no idea what your father looked like. I never met him."

"But—"

Charles Danver stared at me with flat, expressionless eyes, and his voice was granite hard.

"Your mother was a French trollop, a dazzling beauty without a sou to her name although she was descended from one of the noblest families of France. My brother took a grand tour of Europe. He was nearing forty and still unwed. As the eldest son, it was imperative that he produce an heir, unless, of course, he wanted me to inherit. He didn't want that, let me assure you. He met your mother at a watering place outside Paris. He was captivated by her beauty and fell head over heels in love. He asked her to become his wife, even though he had learned she was carrying the child of a military man who had deserted her. They were wed. Five months later, you were born. My brother never sired a child."

"Then—"

"You're a bastard," he said bluntly. "Oh, you bear the name of Danver—George always was a fool, he recognized you as his own—but the fact remains."

If Charles Danver had slapped me across the face, I couldn't have been more stunned. My blood seemed to turn to water, and my knees grew weak. I had to summon all my control to keep from fainting. The man who was not my uncle stared at me with those expressionless eyes, or was there a touch of malice in them? I could not give him the satisfaction of seeing me faint. I squared my shoulders. I held my chin high. I managed to look at him with a cool, level gaze.

"I am not your niece, then," I said.

"In name only."

"Why did you pay for my schooling? Why have you

sent for me? I can't believe it was because of your generous heart."

"A point well taken," he said, flicking ashes into a porcelain tray. "I have not the slightest interest in you as an individual, but you do, unfortunately, bear the name Danver. It is a very important name in London. I have a number of business associates, a number of enemies who are always interested in anything pertaining to Charles Danver."

"I think I understand," I said stiffly.

Charles Danver took the cigar out of his mouth, blowing a wispy plume of blue-gray smoke that curled slowly to the ceiling. A half-smile played on his wide mouth, and his heavy eyelids drooped. I was no longer intimidated, no longer afraid. This interview had been one shock after another, and tremulous apprehension had been replaced by an icy calm.

"As far as the world is concerned, you are my niece," he continued, "and a niece of Charles Danver cannot grow up in an orphanage. I paid for your schooling because it was necessary, and I have brought you to Danver Hall because I could not allow you to seek employment as a governess, although I understand you were prepared to do so."

"I shall," I retorted, "I shall leave this house at once."

"No, my dear," he said, "you shall not. Your true paternity aside, I am, nevertheless, your legal guardian until you are twenty-one years of age. Until that time, you shall do precisely as I say."

His voice was lazy, almost gentle, but there was a lethal undertone. I was helpless, and I had the good sense to realize it. I was his ward, and, Victorian laws being what they were, I had no recourse but to obey him to the letter. I could run away, but where could I go? What could I do? He would track me down, and he would show no mercy in dealing with any rebellion. Of that I was certain.

Charles Danver seemed to be reading my thoughts. He crushed the cigar out, jabbing it brutally against the tray, and folded his arms across his chest. Tilting his chin down, he stared at me, a wave of dark, unruly black hair spilling forward over his brow.

"What do you expect of me?" I asked calmly.

"Complete submission," he replied.

"I have no alternative, have I?"

"None whatsoever," he agreed.

"Am I to be your servant?"

He arched one dark brow in mock surprise. He smiled, thoroughly enjoying his position. He would have liked for me to cringe and cower, but I had far too much pride. Timid I might be, nervous and highly strung, yet I refused to succumb before this man.

"A servant?" he inquired. "My dear, you've been reading far too many cheap novels. You've been brought up as a young gentlewoman, as my niece. You could hardly expect me to banish you to the kitchens."

"I don't know what to expect," I replied.

"You have been brought here as my niece, and you shall be treated as such. You shall dine with my son and me. You shall be shown every courtesy. Anything that you might require—new clothes, pin money—I shall readily provide. Your true parentage is our secret, Jane. No one else knows, not even my son."

"I see."

"I am not quite the arch-villain you imagine me to be."

"No?"

"I am a hard man, true, and many call me unscrupulous. I consider that a compliment. We live in an age where weakness is glorified, hypocrisy is rampant. I am not weak, and I am not a hypocrite. I own one of the finest textile mills in the country. When I inherited it, it was a shambles, producing only a token amount of fabric, and that of inferior quality. I made it what it is today, through strength, through determination. If my employees fear me, if my competitors call me a cutthroat upstart, so much the better. I am interested only in results."

"I'm sure you have reason to be proud," I said acidly, "but I fail to see what that has to do with me."

"If I have been brutal with you, it was because I felt it necessary. The results have been most satisfactory. I wanted you to be fully aware of your position in my house. I believe you are."

"Very much so."

Charles Danver sighed, relieved. He strolled over to the windows and stood peering out at the rain, a large, powerful figure silhouetted against the light. He had explained everything, but I had the feeling that something had been omitted. He had another motive for bringing me to Danver Hall, a motive he had failed to mention. I could not explain why I felt this way, yet the certainty was there.

"I shall, of course, settle a dowry on you," he said, his back to me. "It will be generous enough to induce some chap to marry you. You'll not capture a prize, Jane, but I'll see to it that you eventually find a suitable husband."

He turned around to face me. "Have you nothing to say?"

"I don't imagine anything I might say would make the slightest difference, Mr. Danver."

"Quite true," he said, the sensuous mouth turning up at the corners. "You're an intelligent girl, Jane."

He thrust his large hands into the pockets of his trousers and sauntered over to me. He stood with his legs spread wide apart. His jacket hung open, the plum colored vest stretching tightly across the expanse of chest. I was intensely aware of his brute strength, his potent virility. For all his ruthlessness, Charles Danver was an impressive figure of a man. I had to concede this, no matter what I might think of him. Remarkably well preserved, ruggedly handsome, he had an aura of aggressive force that was almost tangible.

"I know a great deal about you," he said. "Although you never received any direct communication from me, I had a thorough report on your progress each month from the head mistress of your school."

"Indeed?"

"Your marks were excellent from the very first. You showed a remarkable aptitude for intellectual pursuits. Scholastically, your record was above reproach. However, you were seriously lacking in other departments. You were neurotic, sickly, anti-social. You did not get along with the other girls, nor did you make any effort to do so."

That was true enough, I thought, remembering the taunts of my classmates and their frivolities.

"You were subject to severe headaches," he continued. "You were frequently too ill to attend classes. You complained of weariness and lethargy, although there was no apparent reason for it. The doctors were unable to explain it. They finally agreed it was merely another sign of a neurosis. You were unhappy, and you chose this way to express it."

He paused, waiting for me to make some comment, but none was forthcoming. I remembered those dreadful days when I stayed in bed, my bones aching with fatigue, my head throbbing painfully. The exhaustion, the pain had been quite real, but I did not intend to try and justify it to Charles Danver. He could believe whatever he chose to believe.

"I understand, too, that you have no recollection of the first seven years of your life. Partial amnesia, I think they call it."

"That's true," I replied.

"You don't remember this house? You don't remember anything that took place here?"

"I remember nothing whatsoever."

Charles Danver frowned, a deep crease over the bridge of his nose. He found my amnesia puzzling, as did everyone who learned of it. The doctors had been bewildered. My teachers had considered it merely another sign of instability.

"Perhaps your memory will return," he said. "Perhaps being here will help you remember. At any rate, there's nothing so unusual about forgetting one's childhood. I'd be hard pressed to answer many questions about my own early years." He glanced at the windows. "The rain seems to be slacking up. I must go to the mill this morning. There are some important disciplinary measures I have to attend to."

He straightened the lapels of his jacket and adjusted the folds of the buff colored stock, and then he moved over to a desk and picked up a thin leather portfolio. When he turned around, he seemed surprised to see me still standing there. His mind was already on other things.

"I am dismissed?" I inquired.

"You're dismissed," he said irritably. "And . . . one other thing, I'm a busy man. I don't like to be bothered. I've devoted a considerable amount of time to you this morning because it was necessary to get things clear, but don't expect it in the future. If you have any requests to make you are to go through Madame DuBois, my housekeeper. You're free to do as you please, but stay out of the way. Do you understand what I mean?"

"Perfectly."

"Very good," he said brusquely. "Now get out of here."

I left the room far more composed than I had been when I entered. Considering what I had been through, the icy calm was remarkable, but my mind was clearer than it had been for some time. The nervous apprehension, the mental anguish was gone. I was no longer plagued with doubts and fears. The worst had happened, and now I must try to adjust to it. As I moved through the main hall, I saw Madame DuBois standing by the mail table. There was a guileless expression on her face. I knew she had been eavesdropping.

CHAPTER FOUR

I couldn't stay in my room any longer. Yesterday, after the interview with Charles Danver, I had gone directly to my room, staying there until Susie came to announce dinner. My guardian and I dined alone in the lofty, baronial dining room, neither of us making an attempt at conversation. A long, miserable night had passed, and now it was after noon. The room was a haven, but I realized I couldn't stay shut in any longer. The walls were beginning to press in on me. I had to get out. I had to walk and think and come to terms with all that had happened.

Moving down the back hall, I followed the servants' stairs down to the kitchen. It was empty, although there were bustling sounds coming from the pantry. A fire burned in the enormous rough stone fireplace, flames reflecting on the varnished surface of the tall golden oak cupboards and the dark red tile floor. Pots and pans were piled up on the zinc drain board. There was a delicious spicy smell and the fragrance of apples. Cook's sleepy marmalade cat was curled up on a rag rug in front of the hearth, and he peered at me indifferently as I moved across the room. I followed a dark, narrow hallway to the back door and stepped outside.

No one had told me how to reach the back door. I had come instinctively, without directions, without even thinking about it. Realizing this, I paused on the back steps, bewildered. How had I known the way? Was I beginning to remember? Would the rest of my memory return? My head began to throb, and there was a sensation much like fear. Why? Was I *afraid* to remember? I pushed these thoughts out of my mind and moved on down the steps to the gardens.

The sky was a deep pearl color with the faintest touch of blue, strong white sunlight gleaming brightly. The gardens were tattered, dark green shrubs drooping, flowerbeds ragged. The rain had stripped the rose bushes, petals like shreds of pink and red silk scattered over the damp brown soil. To my left, beyond the vegetable gardens, stood the carriage house and the stables, a crushed shell drive in front of them leading around the side of the house. To my right, far away and sheltered by oak trees, Dower House looked neat and serene with sunlight gilding the roof.

I followed the winding flagstone path toward the line of trees in back of the property, passing the lily pond, passing the arbor where honeysuckle grew thickly on weathered white latticework trellises. I was going to the moors. I would find solace there. I sensed that, and I did not question my instincts. The moors seemed to call to me.

Pausing at the trees, I turned to look back at Danver Hall. It was a solid bulk of towering gray walls, heavily leaded windows like dark eyes staring back at me. Stout black smokestacks and sooty red brick chimneys studded the multi-leveled roof, and I could see the twin towers rearing up in front, their rounded stone turrets casting long shadows over the green slate. Bathed in bright sunlight, the west wing looked even more desolate. Why had it never been torn down? Why had it never been closed off? I found this extremely puzzling.

As I stood looking at the house, I saw a curtain move at one of the windows in the east wing, a long, thin face peering out. Although I was too far away to discern features, I knew it was Madame DuBois spying on me. She had been hovering in the hall again last night when Charles Danver and I left the dining room, her face as guileless as it had been on that earlier occasion. She was worried about something. I presented a threat to her, and I knew it wasn't because she was afraid I would discover her relationship with my guardian. No, there was some other reason . . . The curtain fell back in place.

I turned toward the moors, trying to forget the incident.

The land was flat, barren, without a single tree, without a single sign of life, and there was an atmosphere of great age and great mystery. In the distance I could see patches of tarry black bog, stakes driven in the ground at intervals around them to warn one of danger. Those treacherous bogs could swallow a man without leaving a trace. Age old, they probably contained the bones of primeval creatures, I thought, walking slowly up the gradually sloping hill. The wind swept over the land, fierce, swirling into cracks and crevices, speaking in its own harsh voice, but I found it almost comforting. Serenity came, a curious calm induced by this rugged terrain that seemed to welcome me as an old friend. I felt safe, protected, and I knew not why.

At the crest of the hill, I turned around again. Danver Hall was far away now, a tiny gray toy house that some child had broken on one side. I felt as though I had been released from prison, and the feeling was a familiar one. I had felt this way before many years ago. I knew that without actually remembering. I wanted to run, bursting with elation, free again from dreary routine. No piano practice, no governess in starched blue dress, no boring afternoon nap. I stood there with the wind tearing at the skirt of my dark brown dress, concentrating, trying to make these vague impressions take solid shape in my mind.

I couldn't remember. Conscious effort only made it worse.

I moved down the hill. Enormous boulders began to surge up all around me, and I could hear the water. The ground was spongy now, and there were a few stunted trees with twisted limbs and dark green leaves. I moved on, boulders on either side studded with mica that glittered in the strong sunlight. Turning, walking along a well worn pathway, I could see the stream splashing over a rocky bed, and soon I began to see the waterfalls spilling over the boulders in savage cascades, the bank covered with moss. The wind was far away now, but the sound of water filled the valley with music, fierce, discordant music that I knew and loved.

It was fifteen minutes before I found the place. It

was waiting, as I had known it would be. Moving through a wide crevice, I stepped into the small clearing surrounded on three sides by tall boulders. A waterfall fell in noisy silver sprays into the pool, mist glittering in the sunlight, and dark green moss covered the ragged sloping bank. There was my flat boulder, my seat at the edge of the water, and there were the delicate purple flowers growing in the cracks of the gray stone walls. It was my secret place, and I saw a bright, merry child with curly brown hair perched on the rock, dangling her bare legs into the cool water. The impression flashed into my mind and disappeared with lightning speed, but in that instant it had been vividly real.

Spreading my skirt out carefully, I sat down on the rough, flat rock and stared into the pool. I could see my reflection in the water, blurred, shimmering, like one of those new impressionist paintings they were doing in Paris. I listened to the water, and soon the sound vanished and became a mere background, and I heard only those sounds I created in my own mind. Sitting very still, a fine mist from the waterfall spraying over my skirt, I let my mind go, attuned to the place, picking up impressions that seemed to fill the air.

I was a bastard. "Illegitimate" was a more polite way to put it, but Charles Danver had wanted to make his point strongly. Although George Danver had given me his name, I was the daughter of a French trollop and an unidentified military man. I had no reason to believe that my guardian was lying, and yet . . . and yet that child who had sat on this rock had been a happy child. I sensed that. Rebellious, yes, always getting into scrapes as Johnny had put it, yet happy. There had been much love. I could not remember my mother, but I had a distinct impression of someone bright and lovely and gay. I knew that she had loved me. I could almost hear her voice, crooning. What was it she said? "Jane, my little Jane." No, something else, something similar. The memory refused to come, but it was so near, the thinnest veil obscuring it. I had been loved, and happy.

Something had changed all that.

My mind went blank for a moment, and there was darkness and rumbling sounds and it seemed I could see a cloud of dust and hear a scream. I felt the pain, the fear. I closed it out. Quickly, quickly I mentally ran away from that horror waiting just beyond my conscious memory. I could feel the pulses at my temples begin to throb. I pressed them tightly with my fingertips, willing the headache away, refusing to give in to it.

I saw the pale little girl with long braids who stood in the office of the head mistress. The child wore a dull brown dress and a heavy brown coat and carried a heavy suitcase. She was trembling, awed and frightened. Oh yes, I remembered that first day well enough, and I remembered each day that followed. What had transformed the merry child into the drab sparrow? A tragedy had occurred, true, but children are resilient. Children get over such things after a reasonable period of time. I never did. All gaiety was gone forever. Something had happened, and it had been so terrible that it had completely altered my personality.

The accident? Had I seen it happen? Had I seen something else as well?

I thought about Charles Danver and his reason for

sending for me. The name Danver was important, and it would embarrass him if any of his business associates learned he had a niece who had been forced to seek employment. The motive was sound, but was it sound enough to justify bringing me to Danver Hall? He could have made other arrangements for me. Having me in his home was part of some scheme. I was certain of it. There was a reason for my being here, and it wasn't merely to avoid embarrassment. A man like Charles Danver wouldn't have taken such a step unless he had a definite purpose in mind.

What could that purpose be? Was I imagining things? I wasn't given to fancies, nor did I dramatize myself as did so many girls my age. I was cool and logical, and my logic told me that something was wrong.

If only Jamintha were here. I could confide in her. She would listen to me, and she would understand. She would tell me what to do, advise me, share my problems as she had shared them at school.

I sat on the rock for over an hour, lost in thought, staring at the shimmering reflection in the water without seeing it. The waterfall continued to spill over the rock, spray glittering with misty violet and blue and gold facets as it fanned in the air. I stood up, ready to leave now, my mind at ease. I would wait. There was nothing I could do but wait and see what happened. Worrying would not help, nor would fretting about my situation. I must take each day as it came. I resolved to do that.

My skirt was damp from spray, and a few wisps of hair had escaped from their prison to rest lightly on my temples. Moving back through the crevice, I left my private place, but I did not turn back the way I had come. Instead, I continued to follow the well worn path, winding among the enormous stones and eventually reaching the barren ground again. The land was hilly here, rolling with sudden slopes, and there were cracks where the earth had split open. There were gleaming black stretches of peat here too, these unmarked by any stakes, and a few trees grew, stark in the emptiness, twisted into bizarre shapes by the tormenting wind.

I was not lost. I did not consciously know where I was, but I knew I could find my way back to Danver Hall, just as I had found my way to the pool with its mossy bank. I knew this land, responded to it with a part of myself, and years of separation had made no difference. I walked over the rocky slopes, the wind a live thing accompanying me every step of the way, caressing my cheeks with vigorous strokes, lifting my skirts. My braids were beginning to come undone, strands of hair spilling out of place, but I paid no attention. I was not used to this much exercise, but it did not tire me. It seemed, instead, to have the reverse effect. I felt stronger, more certain of myself than I had felt in quite a long time.

There was a distant sound I could not identify, a pounding, rumbling noise, and then a horse galloped over the horizon, startling me. It was a magnificent beast, a black stallion with glossy skin and powerful muscles that rippled as it raced toward me, the heavy hooves kicking up clumps of soil. The saddle was empty, the bridle flapping wildly. The animal seemed bent on trampling me. Stunned, too terrified to cry out, I watched as it sped closer. It reared up not five yards away, snorting viciously, hooves waving in the air, and then it galloped off in another direction, disappearing over a slope. A hand pressed over my rapidly beating heart. Nerves shaken, I listened as the sound of hooves grew fainter and then were gone.

Someone was in trouble. Someone had been thrown out of the saddle. I hurried forward, alarmed. The man might be seriously hurt. A person could die of exposure on these moors. His leg broken, no way of summoning aid, a man could perish. Reaching the slope where the horse had first appeared, I paused, peering in every direction, but there was nothing but desolate land and those treacherous stretches of black. How would I ever find him? What was I going to do?

The groan was quite audible. It came from the narrow gully only a few yards from where I stood. I moved rapidly, and in a moment I was staring down at the man sprawled on the ground. He wore glossy black knee boots and tight gray breeches. A white silk shirt with billowing sleeves and a Byronic collar was open at the throat. His unruly black hair fell in a tangled mass over his forehead, and his eyes were closed. He was even more handsome than two nights before when I had seen him coming out of the pub.

"Are—are you hurt?" I stammered.

The man opened his eyes and stared at me, but I could see that he was not able to focus properly. The eyes were a very vivid blue. They looked glazed. He groaned again and struggled into a sitting position, wincing as he did so. He shook his head and blinked his eyes, and then he peered up at me again. The beautifully shaped mouth curled into a boyish grin. He was obviously drunk.

"Good thing you happened along, wench," he said.

"Are you able to stand? Here, let me help you up."

I reached down for his hand, intending to pull him to his feet. With a boisterous laugh he seized my hand, jerked me into his lap and imprisoned me in strong arms, crushing me against him.

"'Ow about a tumble, lass? No one around to bother us. It's a glorious opportunity, what?"

I struggled violently. He grinned and wound his arms tighter around me, hurting me. His mouth fastened over mine, the firm lips urgent and demanding, and in one quick motion he swerved around until I was flat on the ground, his body on top of mine. Freeing my arms, I pounded his back. I seized his hair, jerking his head, but his lips continued to cover my own with bruising force. The weight of his body pinioned me to the ground. Tiny rocks scraped against my back painfully as I fought.

"Regular wildcat, ain't you?" he said, laughing. Seizing my wrists, he moved into a kneeling position, his buttocks on my stomach, a knee on either side of my thighs.

"Let me go!" I cried. "You—"

"Aw, don't carry on so," he said amiably. "You know you're enjoyin' it."

The vivid blue eyes gleamed with delight, and the wide, sensual mouth curved up in a devilish smile. I was terrified, the blood racing through my veins, my breath coming in short, frantic gasps. His silk shirt was damp, clinging to his chest, and the smell of alcohol was overwhelming. I squirmed and struggled, trying to throw him off, but his hands gripped my wrists tightly, the fingers like steel. I stared up at that handsome face, my eyes full of horror.

JAMINTHA

"You're a lucky lass, you are," he taunted. "Come on now, don't put on such a show. I might hafta get rough."

He released one of my wrists and reached for the hem of my skirt, and I swung my free hand with all the force I could muster. It struck his face with such impact that he toppled over sideways. I jumped to my feet, and he stared up at me with a stunned expression. He sat up again and shook his head vigorously. I backed away, my heart beating rapidly.

"My God," he whispered, seeing me clearly for the first time. "You're not one of the village lasses."

"Indeed not!" I said hoarsely.

"You're—my God! I know who you are."

"And I know who you are!"

I should have guessed it from the first, of course. Brence Danver had been described to me on at least three different occasions. He was, indeed, as handsome as Satan before the Fall, and he was certainly a blighter. With great effort I managed to compose myself. I stared at him with loathing, and he looked up at me in wonderment.

"I must-a been blind," he said.

"Blind drunk, more likely," I retorted crisply.

"No harm done, Cousin Jane."

"No harm done! You almost—"

"Shut up!" he ordered gruffly, scowling. "You'll survive. My head is splittin', and my body feels like I've been chunked out the window of a tower. Christ! That damned horse—I should-a had better sense than try 'n ride him in my condition. I thought a brisk ride'ud help—"

"You certainly can't expect any sympathy from me," I said, my voice pure acid.

"Stop your blabbin'. You would-a loved it."

"How dare you—"

"I said shut up!"

He glared at me, brows lowered. His sculptured cheekbones were pale, and there were deep smudges under his eyes. His forehead glistened with dampness, strands of hair clinging wetly, and a muscle at the corner of his mouth twitched. He looked frightfully ill now that the effects of the liquor were wearing off. Trembling with rage, I glared at him.

"Don't just stand there with your back stiff as a poker," he snapped angrily. "Help me up."

"I wouldn't dream of it, Mr. Danver."

"God, you are a little priss, aren't-ja? I think I've twisted my ankle. It's throbbing somethin' awful. You can't just march off and leave me here."

"That's precisely what I intend to do."

"Listen," he growled, "I realize I almost committed a terrible blunder, but I wasn't seein' too well. If I'd-a had a good look at your face I wouldn't-a laid a finger on you."

"You're no gentleman, Mr. Danver."

"That's for damned sure, an' you're no beauty, Cousin Jane. God, I must'uv been smashed!"

He tried to get to his feet, but as soon as he put weight on his left foot his face contorted with pain. I could see that he was really hurt, and I knew I couldn't walk off and leave him in this condition. He stared up at me, waiting. I drew back, reluctant to go near him.

He frowned savagely. "Well?" he said impatiently.

"I'll help you get back to the house," I said primly.

"Damned decent of you," he retorted in a sullen voice.

I extended my hand. Holding on to it with both his own, he managed to pull himself up, hopping on one foot. We took a few steps and then he stopped and grimaced, trying to keep the agony out of his eyes. His forehead was beaded with perspiration now, and his face was chalk white.

"I don't think we're going to make it," he informed me. His voice was laced with pain, but it was no longer slurred.

"Perhaps I could find the horse—"

"He's probably already back at the stables by now."

"Then we'll make it on our own," I replied calmly.

"I'm not so sure. God! Look, I'll have to have more support. You're going to have to practically carry me."

"I'll do what I can."

He slung his heavy arm around my shoulder, almost stumbling as he did so. His forearm hung across my bosom. Reaching for his wrist, I held it in a firm grasp, winding my other arm around his waist. We started our curious progress across the moor. He just managed to hobble along with me supporting most of his weight. His eyes were closed. He was almost delirious with pain, but still we progressed. His body was warm, reeking with perspiration and the smell of liquor, and I nearly stumbled several times myself under the weight of my burden. Brence Danver was silent except for an occasional moan.

We walked for perhaps twenty minutes. I had to stop for a while. He understood, nodding his head and pointing to a small flat boulder. We managed to reach it, and I helped him ease himself down onto the rock. He sat with his hands resting on his knees.

His hair was plastered to his skull in wet locks, and his face was dripping. Sore myself, almost too weak to stand after the terrific effort it had taken to get this far, I nevertheless tore a piece off my petticoat and wiped his face.

"Leave me alone," he said gruffly. "I don't want you coddling me."

"You have a fever. You're shivering."

"It's the liquor, luv. I drank damned near a whole bottle this morning."

"Why would you do a thing like that?" I asked, appalled.

"You wouldn't understand," he muttered.

"Surely you must realize what you're doing to your health."

"Don't preach, Cousin."

"You're a fool, Mr. Danver."

"Yeah, and you're a bloody little prig."

He closed his eyes, too weak to say anything more. I wiped his face thoroughly and brushed the damp black locks away from his forehead. His shirt, soaked with perspiration, was clinging to his skin, and he continued to shiver in the wind. I was deeply worried, realizing how urgent it was to get him back to the house as quickly as possible. Eyes closed, his cheeks flushed a feverish pink now, Brence Danver moaned. His lips were dry, the skin beginning to chap. It was hard to believe he was the same man who had pulled me into his arms a short time ago.

After a few minutes I helped him up and we started off again, his arm looped around my shoulder as before, his big body sagging, leaning heavily on me. It was difficult going, and Brence Danver was giving me no help at all now. I was half dragging him, certain that my knees would give way at any moment. Every step was a strain, and it was painful, but there were other sensations I couldn't properly identify. I should have been repelled by his touch, but the sensations were almost . . . almost pleasant.

He stumbled over a rock, crying out in pain, swerving around and flinging his other arm around me to keep from falling. I held him up, my arms around his back, and he clung to me like a child, barely conscious. His head rested on my shoulder, his sagging body flattened against me, both his arms curled tightly around my shoulders. An onlooker would have thought us lovers locked in a passionate embrace, I thought, blushing. I could feel his heart pounding, and his skin seemed to be on fire. Raising his head, Brence Danver winced.

"Sorry, luv," he said in a hoarse whisper. "You must have hated that."

"I—are you able to go on?"

"I wish you'd left me there to die," he muttered.

"Don't be melodramatic," I said stiffly.

He managed a weak, sarcastic smile and hobbled around to my side again. It was perhaps half an hour before I saw Danver Hall in the distance. I don't think Brence was really conscious. His eyes were closed, and he moved like a sleepwalker in the middle of a feverish nightmare. Holding him tightly, every muscle in my body aching, I staggered on toward the trees that stood like sentinels, separating the gardens from the moor.

I heard a loud retort in the distance, like a door slamming, and in a moment I saw Susie racing toward us, her faded pink skirt billowing like wings, her dark golden hair flying in the wind. Reaching us, she didn't say a word. She took his free arm and swung it around her shoulder, helping me support him. Brence groaned, his dry lips twisting in pain, but he had no idea what was happening. Susie and I got him through the trees and moved him along the flagstone path, past the lily pond, past the vegetable gardens. We paused at the foot of the back steps.

"I was looking out the kitchen windows and saw you coming," Susie said in a calm voice. "The horse came back alone. I'm not surprised. Master Brence was frightfully tipsy when he took off this afternoon."

We dragged him up the steps. His ankle knocked against one of them, and he cried out sharply, his body stiffening. Susie opened the back door and we moved him down the hall and into the vast drawing room. A fire was burning in the fireplace. We put Brence on the long green sofa. He sprawled out, sinking heavily against the cushions, the injured ankle dangling over the side.

"Mister Charles is still at the mill," Susie said. "Madame is in her apartment. Shall I fetch her?"

"I think not," I said in a firm voice, and I could see that Susie approved. She nodded and moved briskly out of the room.

I lifted his head and arranged a cushion under it. He groaned, jerking his head away, and I wondered why I was so calm, so serene. I should have been crumpling with exhaustion after the ordeal, but I seemed to be charged with energy and determination. Susie returned promptly with a bottle of pure alcohol, cloths, a towel and a blue and black striped satin dressing robe which she must have fetched from his room. Placing the things on a table, she regarded

JAMINTHA

me with a cool, efficient gaze, her hands on her hips.

"If you can manage alone, Miss Jane, I'll take the mare and ride to the village for Doctor Green. I imagine we'll be needing him."

"Of course," I said.

She left immediately. A few minutes later I heard a horse galloping around the side of the house. Bending over him, I pulled the damp shirt out of his waistband and shoved it gently up over his chest. Sliding my arm under his broad shoulders and lifting him up, I was able to get the garment over his head, pulling his arms free. I took the towel and dried him off. His naked torso was lean and muscular, his skin a light tan and the texture of silk. I blushed, averting my eyes as much as possible. Brence moaned as I pulled him into a sitting position. Slipping his arms into the sleeves of the robe, I wrapped it around him and tied the sash loosely. In a few moments I had him propped against several cushions and began to remove the boot.

It was difficult. The ankle had swollen. I tugged and pulled, trying not to hurt him any more than was absolutely necessary. He groaned, thrashing his head. I saw that this method wasn't going to work. Gripping the boot firmly, I gave one savage jerk, almost falling over as it came free. Brence Danver screamed in anguish, sitting up with a start, his eyes wide open. He cursed me, using words I had never heard before, and then he fell back against the cushions in a dead faint.

I bathed the foot in alcohol, handling the bruised flesh with care. I wrapped it tightly with one of the cloths Susie had brought. The doctor would bandage it properly later on. Pulling a chair over to the sofa, I sat down beside it and watched him as the clock ticked slowly. He was sleeping peacefully now, and his brow didn't feel so feverish. Almost an hour passed before Susie returned with the doctor.

"It's merely a sprain," the doctor said, examining the ankle. "He'll be able to walk on it in a day or so."

"He had a terrible fever—" I began.

"Not at all surprised," the doctor said brusquely, taking bandages out of his bag. "I can still smell the liquor. How much did he drink, do you know?"

"Almost a bottle."

"Hmph! He'll kill himself one of these days. He's been warned."

"Has he—has he always drunk so much?" I asked hesitantly.

"He went on his first binge at seventeen. Hasn't stopped since."

Doctor Green, at least, was one person who wasn't afraid of the Danvers. He certainly had no reservations about speaking his mind, frankly and without professional niceties. He began to bandage the foot, handling it none too gently. Susie assisted him, and I stood in front of the fireplace, cringing every time the doctor's rough treatment made Brence groan. Doctor Green finished up and began to repack his bag.

"Don't try to move him tonight. Let him sleep it off. He'll feel like hell in the morning, but the worst is over."

"He'll be all right?"

"Until the next time," he retorted.

Susie showed the doctor out and returned to the drawing room.

"I'll fetch some blankets and put another log on

the fire," she said. "He'll sleep comfortably the rest of the night. You'd better go on up to your room now, Miss Jane. You must be exhausted."

"Yes. I—I suppose I am."

I went to my room. I washed and changed into a fresh dress. As I brushed my hair and braided it, I seemed to be in a trance. I was suffused with new sensations that seemed to glow inside. I tried to ignore them. I tried to deny them. It was futile. Bewildered, alarmed, completely horrified, I realized that I had fallen in love with Brence Danver.

CHAPTER FIVE

A week passed. I did not see him even once. He had not dined with us, but I knew that he was up and about. Susie had informed me of this, adding that his ankle was as good as new and no one would guess he'd ever sprained it. It was a long week, and during those days I mastered my emotions, banishing the love I couldn't deny. It was a futile love, and I had enough good sense to realize it. It was still there, still very much alive, but it would be kept deeply inside. Perhaps, if I were lucky, it would suffocate and vanish entirely. Cool, reserved, prim, I would never allow myself to acknowledge it again.

When it was not raining, I walked on the moors, frequently staying away for several hours, and when the weather would not permit it I stayed in my room re-reading the few books I had brought with me. I was restless, and I was lonely. Susie was a bright, cheerful companion, but she took her duties seriously and they kept her occupied most of the day. Charles Danver and I dined together every night, and there was a strained politeness between us. He found me dull and uninteresting and made little effort to conceal it. I avoided Helene DuBois whenever possible. I felt that the woman was constantly spying on me, and I couldn't understand why. What did she expect me to do?

It was raining on Monday morning. Susie brought in my breakfast and stayed a while to chatter about Johnny. She had seen him the night before, and I knew that she must have slipped out of the house to do so. She admitted as much, saying that what she did after hours was her own business and those as didn't like it could lump it. Johnny waited for her in his wagon in the woods just beyond Danver Hall. Her lively brown eyes were full of anticipation as she described the Danver County fair that was to be held in just a few weeks' time. There would be tents and booths and a wooden dance floor and a bonfire and ever so many exciting things to see and do. Johnny was going to take her, *if* he behaved himself in the meantime. If not, she would go with Randy Stevens. Randy had smouldering brown eyes and wavy black hair and an attractive smile and was, actually, a much better catch than Johnny, though he was sometimes hard to manage.

"Will you be going to the fair, Miss Jane?" she inquired, brushing a lock of dark golden hair from her temple.

"I don't imagine so," I replied.

"Mister Charles will be there, of course. He's one of the judges. And Master Brence *always* goes. He'll probably get into another fight, like he did last year. You really should go, Miss Jane. You'd enjoy it, I know, and it'd do you *good*."

I made no comment. I listened to the rain splattering on the rooftop and spilling off the eaves. It was a monotonous sound, depressing. Susie sensed my mood. She frowned, concerned.

"Are you going to stay in your room again today?" she asked, gathering up the breakfast things. "All that reading! It'd drive me stark raving mad, an' that's no lie."

"I've run out of things to read," I said.

"Lands! There must be *millions* of books in the library. No one ever reads 'em."

"I didn't know Danver Hall had a library."

"Oh, it's closed up. Filled with dust and cobwebs. Mister Charles doesn't care anything about it, and as for Master Brence—can you imagine *him* with a book in his hand? There are over thirty rooms in the house, you know, more than half of 'em closed up, dust covers over all the furniture. Who's there to keep 'em *up*, I'd like to know? Cook and I have a hard time as it is."

"I'd like to see the library."

"Spooky place," Susie said, tray in hand.

She gave me directions and informed me I'd have to obtain the key from Madame DuBois. After Susie had gone, I finished my ablutions and changed into a dark blue dress, finally leaving the room. I eventually located Madame DuBois in the drawing room. She looked up sharply as I entered.

"Yes?" she said coldly.

"I'd like the key to the library," I told her.

"The library? I'm afraid it's closed up, Miss Danver. No one uses it any longer."

"I'm aware of that. The key, please."

"I'm sure your uncle wouldn't want you prowling around in there," she said in a cold, level voice. "It could even be dangerous. The woodwork has rotted. The galleries aren't safe."

"I'm afraid I must insist you give me the key."

She hesitated, wanting to defy me, not certain how far she should go. She was in full make-up and her dress, an apple green taffeta with beige velvet ribbons, was frilly, old fashioned and madly unsuitable for a housekeeper. She was a bizarre figure, yet there was a hard, steely quality that couldn't be ignored. I wondered what my guardian could possibly see in her. Perhaps her chief attraction was one of availability. She was on hand, convenient. Or was it something else? Could she possibly have some hold over him?

Helene DuBois took the key from her ring and handed it to me.

"I would advise you to be careful, Miss Danver," she said. "There could easily be an accident. The galleries are rotten, as I have said. The wooden columns that helped support them were removed years ago. The shelves are no longer sturdy, either. They could topple over."

"Thank you for warning me," I replied.

I could feel her watching me as I left the room.

The library was on the west side of the house, in the front corner of the main portion. I shivered as I moved down a long, icy corridor. This section was obviously closed up, plaster flaking from the unpapered walls, the sour smell of dust and mildew in the air. I turned a corner and located the huge mahogany doors. The lock was rusty, and it was some time before I could get the key to turn. The doors finally swung slowly open with a loud, raspy creak as I pushed them all the way back and stepped inside. I stared at the room in amazement.

It was enormous, three stories high, three walls composed entirely of bookshelves that loomed all the way up to the ceiling. The shelves were solidly packed with heavy, musty books, thousands upon thousands, and there were two wooden galleries running around them, one on the second floor level, one on the third. On the fourth side of the room was a huge black marble fireplace, tall windows on either side of it. The dusty purple drapes were opened, a feeble amount of light coming in. The furniture was covered with sheets, the white cloth gray with age and dust, and cobwebs hung from two large brass chandeliers dangling midway between ceiling and floor. The air was fetid, musty, and there was an odor of damp leather and glue and yellowing paper and dust, dust everywhere.

I knew this room.

There was something in the air, a thick, heavy atmosphere almost palpable, and it had an immediate effect on me. My pulses leaped, and then they seemed to vanish altogether, leaving me in a numb, trance-like state. A voice was speaking to me, felt, not heard, and I strained, listening, trying to comprehend. I stared at the walls of books, shelves sagging under their weight, and I seemed to be staring through a wavering, semi-transparent veil. *You know,* the voice said, *remember, remember,* and then I saw the little girl with a handful of stars and I felt dizzy and I saw the set of books bound in battered tan and brown leather. Gibbon. *The Decline and Fall of the Roman Empire.* The images flashed in my mind, taunting me, dissolving before I could grasp them.

Go ahead, Jane, the voice whispered. *It's there . . .*

I gazed up at the wooden galleries running around

three sides of the room. There was no staircase, no apparent way to reach the galleries. How was one to reach the books on the second and third levels? I moved without actually being aware of it. Something seemed to be pulling me, leading me over to the southwest corner of the room. I stopped in front of the shelf, peering at the books without seeing them, and then I ran my hand down the wood, locating the tiny knob, pressing it, stepping back. There was a heavy groaning noise, and dust spilled down and floated in the air as the shelf swung outward.

I stepped into the tower. It was a vast circular hollow with a rickety iron spiral staircase curling up into the darkness. Eddies of cold, clammy air swirled around me as I started up the staircase, my footsteps ringing on the flat metal steps, echoing up and reverberating against the circular stone walls. There were tiny slit windows, invisible from outside, letting in just enough light to prevent total darkness. The walls were damp, festooned with dark green fungus, and the air was as cold as ice water. Slowly, moving like a sleepwalker, I climbed, passing the first landing. My skirts rustled with the sound of whispers as I climbed on up to the second landing and stopped. My head was throbbing, and my heart beat rapidly as I groped along the stone wall in the semi-darkness.

I pressed the knob. Groaning like a live thing, the wall swung slowly outward, unseen hinges creaking raspily. Directly in front of me now was the wooden gallery. I moved out onto it. On one side were the shelves, on the other was a frail wooden railing and dust-filled air. The gallery was not wide, no more than five feet across, and the floorboards seemed to dip as I walked across them. The books up here were damp with mildew, literally falling apart, and cobwebs hung down from the ceiling, swinging lightly in the currents of air coming from the tower. I moved along, oblivious to the dangerously creaking wood, oblivious to the cobwebs, and my heart pounded painfully.

Go on, Jane, go on, the voice urged me. Although I couldn't really hear the words, I sensed them, and I sensed the urgency. There was a loud tearing sound as though nails were being pulled from the wall, and I felt the floor shaking under my feet.

"What in *hell* are you doing up there!"

Something snapped. Black wings rushed over me, and I closed my eyes, my knees growing weak. I swayed, seizing the railing, and then the darkness lifted and I came awake with a start. I was stunned, petrified with fear. I realized where I was, but I had no idea how I had come to be there.

"Have you lost your bloody *mind!*" Brence Danver yelled.

Space yawned before me, a frail railing all that separated me from it. Waves of dizziness sweeping over me, I peered down through the shadows. I could barely see his upturned face far below. I gripped the railing, my knuckles white. I was trembling violently, and the dizziness increased, causing my head to whirl. I was going to faint. I tried to call out, but no sound would come.

"*Christ!*" he yelled. "Don't move. Don't make a move!"

I closed my eyes again. I was in a whirling void, currents of clammy air sweeping over me, my body beginning to grow limp. I could see myself hurtling through space and crashing to the floor two stories below. I willed myself to hold on. My hands grew damp with perspiration. The wooden railing seemed to slip and slide under my palms. I could hear footsteps ringing with a sharp, metallic clang in the tower, but the sound was far, far away, drowned out by the sound of blood rushing in my veins.

He stepped onto the gallery. It seemed to tilt forward and down, pulling away from the wall.

"Let go of the railing," he said. His voice was level, but there was a note of panic barely under control.

I opened my eyes cautiously. My shoulders were trembling. I looked out at the great empty space and down at the floor so far below. I could see the tattered carpet and the ghostly white shapes of covered furniture. The gallery seemed to sway under my feet as he took another step.

"Let go of the railing!" he repeated, no longer trying to conceal the panic. "Move back against the wall. Move carefully."

"I—I can't," I whispered hoarsely.

Still gripping the railing with moist hands, I turned my head to look at him. He was thirty feet away, edging toward me with his body against the wall of shelves. Rotten lumber creaked with protest against his weight. A board splintered under his foot, pieces crashing down. He grabbed hold of the shelves to keep from falling. Several books tumbled down, great clouds of dust rising like smoke. Brence Danver coughed, clinging to the shelf. His face was white, the skin stretched tautly over those magnificent cheekbones.

"Don't—" I said. "You'll fall—"

He grimaced, dark blue eyes glaring at me. He

took a deep breath and let go of the shelf, turning around so that his back was against it. Stepping over the books and the splintered floorboard, he edged along another ten feet. The gallery sagged. I could feel it pulling away from the wall. Brence stopped, his shoulders hunched up against the shelf.

"Please," I whispered. "Go back."

"Shut up!"

I was paralyzed, too terrified to move. At any second the gallery was going to tear completely away from the wall, hurling us both to the floor in a shower of splintered wood. Brence closed his eyes and continued to edge along. His white shirt was covered with dust.

He was no more than six feet away now. He leaned against the shelves, his chest heaving. It was several seconds before he could catch his breath. He stared at me with vivid blue eyes. I could see him trying to master his own fear.

"Let go of the railing," he said firmly. "Move back against the wall very slowly."

"I—I can't do it. I can't move. My knees—"

"Do as I say!" he shouted.

I turned loose of the railing. My knees buckled. I pitched forward with a faint cry, darkness claiming me. My arm seemed to be pulling out of the socket. I crashed back against the shelf as he jerked me away from the void. He held me, pressing his body against mine as books spilled down from the shelves with choking explosions of dust. The gallery rocked and swayed and grew still. I could feel his heart thumping.

"We're going to edge back to the door," he said quietly. "I'll hold on to your hand."

"I can't do it," I whispered. "I almost fell. I—"

"Listen, you bloody little fool, I've risked my neck to get this far. You'll do exactly as I say, do you understand?"

"Let me go. Save yourself—"

"Stop being melodramatic! If it were going to fall, it would have fallen already. There's no real danger now that you're away from the railing. I'm going to lead you to the staircase, luv, or I'm going to slap you unconscious and *carry* you. Which will it be?"

"I—I'll try," I said meekly.

He flattened himself against the wall and reached for my hand, gripping it tightly as he began to move. His strong hand seemed to crush my own. Flesh and bones folded up painfully under that grip, but I was hardly aware of it. The floor sagged, groaning and creaking with each step we took.

"Watch out for the hole," he said sternly.

There was a hole about two feet square where the floorboard had fallen through, the edges jagged with splinters, tattered books around it. Brence moved on, pulling me along beside him. The door was twelve feet away now, and the floor was sturdier there. We moved more quickly. He stepped through the opening and gave my arm a savage jerk, pulling me after him. I flung my free hand out, accidentally touching the knob. The bookshelf creaked loudly, closing behind us.

"Now! I want an explanation of—"

That was all I heard when the darkness closed in, smothering me . . .

I opened my eyes cautiously, my head aching with a dull, throbbing pain. I was lying on an overstuffed brown velvet sofa with worn, shiny nap. The room was snug, intimate, a small study with a rolltop desk, a large, comfortable chair that matched the sofa and a tall golden oak bookcase bulging with beautifully bound volumes. A fire burned in the sooty white marble fireplace across from the sofa. The Persian carpet had faded blue and gold and black patterns, and dark blue curtains hung at the single window. I sat up, moaning softly, wondering where I was.

Brence Danver stepped into the room, closing the door behind him. He had washed and changed into a fresh white silk shirt and gray trousers. His black hair was disheveled, one curling wave draped over his brow.

"You're awake, I see," he said brusquely.

"Where are we?"

"My retreat. This is where I do my drinking. I think it used to be your father's study. Those are his books."

"How did I—"

"You fainted. I carried you here."

"You *carried* me?"

"You blacked out completely. I almost broke my back getting you here. I didn't think you'd want anyone else to know about your little escapade so I slung you across my shoulders."

"You told no one?"

"It's our secret," he said.

I sat up, brushing my skirt down primly. The skirt was covered with dust, and I could feel patches of it on my damp cheeks. A braid had fallen undone, loops of hair spilling down over the nape of my neck. I knew I must look like a dirty urchin. Brence pulled a handkerchief out of his pocket and handed it to me.

"Thank you," I said.

He stepped over to the desk and rolled the top back, revealing an array of bottles and several glasses. He uncapped a bottle and poured a sparkling amber liquid into a glass while I wiped my cheeks and tried to fasten the braid back in place with the pins that hung loose.

"Drink this," he ordered, thrusting the glass into my hand.

I stared at it with horror, my eyes wide.

"I have never touched spirits," I said, "and I don't intend to start now—"

"Drink it!" he bellowed.

I gulped the liquor down hastily, emptying the glass in what must have been record time. Brence Danver watched me with a stern expression, but I could tell that he was amused. His lips curled up slightly at the corners, and he seemed to be holding back laughter. I set the empty glass down on the floor, lurching forward a little. Smooth liquid fire seemed to course through my veins, and the sensation was not at all unpleasant.

"I think I'm drunk," I said in a faraway voice.

"The way you belted that down, luv, you'll probably pass out again."

"You're mocking me, Mr. Danver."

"That bother you?"

"You're a detestable person."

"That's a helluva thing to say to someone who just saved your life."

"You—what happened?"

"I was passing through the main hall. I thought I heard a noise in the library. I got there just in time to see you walking along the gallery as though it were solid ground. You moved like you were in a trance, luv. I thought you'd fall for sure when I yelled at you."

I didn't say anything. The room seemed to spread, the walls expanding and waving like the sides of a tent. Colors and shapes blurred and merged together as dizziness overcame me, and it was a moment before I could focus properly. The spinning sensations diminished and I could see clearly, but I still felt lightheaded. Everything seemed cozy and warm. I wanted to go to sleep.

"I've seen plenty-a damnfool things in my life," Brence Danver continued, "but that was the damndest, the most foolish. What the hell were you doing in the library, and what the hell were you doing up *there?*"

"I don't know," I said quietly.

"You don't *know!*"

"I—something seemed to call me. I don't remember going up there. I was standing in the middle of the room, and then—and then you were yelling at me."

"How did you know about the hidden staircase?"

"Please leave me alone," I said.

Brence Danver stared at me, his hands resting lightly on his thighs, and then he stepped over to the big brown velvet chair and plopped down in it, swinging one long leg over the arm. The vivid blue eyes continued to peer at me with intensity. He seemed to expect me to go berserk and run screaming from the room.

"The old man said you were neurotic," he said casually. "Personally, I think you're slightly mad. A person who'd do a damnfool thing like that ought to be put away."

The lazy, nonchalant way in which he spoke them gave the words even more sting. I could feel my cheeks flaming and was barely able to restrain the extremely unladylike retort that sprang to mind.

"Tell me," he said, "do you have these spells often?"

"To my knowledge it has never happened before," I replied. My voice was as prim and controlled as I could have hoped, despite the anger and the fuzzy effects of the alcohol.

"To your knowledge? That's not very specific, is it? I understand you have a rather faulty memory. Hell, it could happen all the time and *you* still wouldn't know it."

"You have no right to speak to me in that manner, Mr. Danver, *nor* do you have a right to pass any kind of judgment. If anyone should be put away, it's you. Your conduct is—is—"

"Dastardly?" he suggested.

"Deplorable!" I snapped.

"I suppose you're referring to the episode on the moors."

"I am indeed."

"I guess I should thank you. If you hadn't brought me back like you did, I might have died, I suppose."

"That wouldn't have been such a great loss," I said acidly. The anger seemed to have counteracted all the effects of the alcohol. Everything was sharp and clear.

"So the timid mouse has spirit? I like that. No, it wouldn't have been much of a loss, I confess, though a lot of ladies would have mourned for their handsome fellow. Still, it was rather grand of you to go to all that trouble. What exactly happened that afternoon?"

"You don't remember?"

"I remember getting on Sable and racing over the moors, and I seem to remember lying in a gully and feelin' like death, but everything else is a bit dim. Foggy as hell, in fact."

"Tell me," I said politely, "do you have these spells often?"

"Touché! Point well taken. I have 'em damn near every day. Vaguely, just vaguely, I remember making some sort of dreadful blunder. Was it a whopper?"

"I don't care to discuss it."

He grinned. It was a most engaging grin. I had a suspicion that he knew very well what had happened and was merely taunting me. My cheeks were still blazing, and I stood up with all the dignity I could summon, intending to march briskly out of the room. To my amazement, my knees turned to rubber and I toppled back down on the couch, my head spinning again. Brence Danver chuckled, eyes aglow with amusement.

"You're enjoying this!" I snapped. "You enjoy tormenting people. You are a bully, Mr. Danver, and—"

"And you're beginning to bore me," he said in a flat voice.

The amusement was gone, and his expression turned surly. The silence between us grew heavy. I had the feeling he had forgotten all about me and was dwelling in a world of private torment. Brence Danver was an enigma. For some reason, I felt sorry for him.

"How is your ankle?" I asked timidly.

"It was merely a light sprain," he replied, sullen.

"I'm glad it has healed properly. I was worried—"

"Ah, yes, you were a noble little nurse, bringing me

back to the house and taking care of me until the doctor came. Do you want me to pin a medal on you?"

"I want you to leave this room!" I retorted angrily.

Brench Danver stood up. He seemed to tower over me. The eyes were dark with genuine anger now, and I knew I had gone too far. He was a violent, brooding man with quicksilver moods that could shift without warning. The light, jesting Brence was gone, and in his place was the savage brute who had slapped the barmaid to her knees and sauntered off without a backward glance.

"I don't like your attitude," he said coldly. "I don't like the things you say or the tone you employ when you say them. Women don't speak to me like that."

"You don't know any respectable women," I retorted.

"The women I associate with know their place, Cousin, and they're *women*, not prim, stiff, uppity little schoolgirls. Let's get one thing straight: I don't know why my father sent for you and I couldn't care less, but your position is tenuous. Your name is Danver, but you're not one of *us*. You'll show the proper respect when you speak to me, Cousin, or I'll know the reason why."

"If you think—"

"No back talk! Christ, what a poor excuse for a woman. You're plain and dull, and you're a bloody little fool to boot! In the future, stay out of the library, and stay out of my way. The next time I see you I might not be so patient!"

He charged out of the room, slamming the door

behind him. I sat on the sofa and watched the tiny orange flames devouring the log. The fire glowed brightly and golden sparks shot up the flue. Time passed. The log turned to ashes. The flames vanished, and the room grew cold. It was a long time before I had strength enough to leave.

CHAPTER SIX

There was so much I couldn't understand, so much that bewildered me. Danver Hall and its inhabitants were a perpetual mystery. Even when she wasn't in sight, I felt that Madame DuBois was spying on me, waiting just around the curve of the staircase, standing just beyond the shadows. It didn't make sense, and yet I had the distinct impression that she was lurking about every time I left my room. It was almost as though the woman were waiting for me to make some specific move and expected me to lead her to something. Perhaps I was imagining it, but the impression was unquestionably there.

Brence Danver was puzzling, too. Several days had passed since he took me to the study, and I had avoided him. He dined with us only once, sulking at the table, toying with his food, ignoring me completely and answering his father's remarks in a surly, belligerent manner that caused Charles Danver to scowl. The air was charged with tension. When my guardian suggested that his son accompany him on an inspection of the textile mill the next day, Brence merely smiled a sarcastic smile and said he had other plans. His father fumed, but he did not insist. He arched a heavy eyebrow and took a sip of wine.

"Business has been a bit slow of late," he said calmly. "I think it might be necessary to cut down on your allowance."

"Do that," Brence said, getting to his feet. His dark blue eyes were brilliant, glittering with hatred.

"You think I won't?" Charles Danver said heavily.

Both of them seemed to have forgotten my presence. I might have been invisible, or so insignificant as to be unworthy of notice. I sat nervously, hands clenched in my lap. Brence folded up his napkin and dropped it on the table, making the gesture seem like a challenge.

"I think you won't," he replied.

"Son—"

"I have an appointment in the village," Brence said.

He left the room without another word. Charles Danver turned slightly pale. His hands on the table tightened into fists. It took him a moment to master his rage, and then he, too, left the room. Alone at the enormous table, candles flickering and casting shadows on the lofty walls, I stared at my plate trying to puzzle out the tense drama just enacted between father and son.

Brence Danver obviously hated his father. If so, why didn't he leave Danver Hall? Was it merely because of money? Was he so spineless that he was afraid to try and make a go of it without his father's allowance? Susie seemed to think so. I shamelessly questioned her, and she felt no qualms about gossiping freely.

"Mister Charles wants Master Brence to take an interest in the mill," she said, fluffing the pillows on my bed and tucking the counterpane in place. "Master Brence will take over one of these days, you see, and his father wants him to be prepared."

"That seems reasonable," I remarked.

"Master Brence has other ideas. He hates the mill with a passion. He wants to go to London and lead the life of a fashionable rake—he would be good at that, I 'spect—but Mister Charles refuses to give him the money. They're always arguing about it."

"He's a grown man. He shouldn't expect his father to—"

"Oh, he doesn't want Mister Charles' money," she interrupted. "He wants what's rightfully his—at least he *says* it's his. When his mother died, she left everything to Master Brence, quite a sum, I understand, but it's all tied up in stocks and bonds and Mister Charles has control of 'em. Won't let Master Brence lay a finger on 'em. 'When you've proven yourself responsible enough to handle it, I'll be glad to hand everything over to you,' he says. He knows Master Brence would squander it immediately."

"I imagine he would," I said.

I understood the situation more fully now, and I had to side with my guardian. Brence Danver certainly wasn't responsible enough to handle any large amount of money. His father was merely trying to protect him by withholding it. Brence seemed hellbent on a course of self-destruction, and his father was trying to restrain him as much as possible. Still, the inevitable "Why?" remained. Why was Brence so tormented? What drove him to such excesses? Was it because he had lost his mother at such an early age? Was it because his boyhood had been without love or a sense of security? He seemed to have everything, yet he was as a man possessed by demons.

Something else puzzled me. I knew that Charles Danver must be an extremely wealthy man. He could have afforded to live in the finest house. Why, then, did he remain at Danver Hall? Although the rooms currently in use were in good enough condition, the place was totally unsuitable. It had been built for a vast, sprawling family, and it was much too large. The west wing was in ruins, never repaired, and so many of the rooms were closed up, abandoned to dust and decay. Danver Hall was a relic of times past, uncomfortable, drafty, impossible to heat or keep up properly. Why did Charles Danver hang on to it? It seemed illogical.

It couldn't be family pride. If that were the case, he wouldn't have left the west wing in ruins. He wouldn't have let the rest of the house sink into such a pitiful state of disrepair. No, Charles Danver took no pride in Danver Hall, yet he remained here when he could have built a much more suitable dwelling. There was a mystery here. The house seemed to hold some dark, forbidding secret, and I sensed that it was somehow connected with the tragic accident that had happened eleven years ago.

Something was going to happen. The house itself seemed to be waiting, holding back. I felt it as I wandered through the rooms. The walls seemed to watch me, and there was a tension in the air. I could not shake the feeling that I had been brought here for some purpose, that I was to play an important part in some drama as yet unfolded. That feeling hovered over me, always there, even though day followed day and I was virtually ignored by the other members of the household.

I thought about what had happened in the library. Something had drawn me there. The room had been waiting for me. I couldn't explain why I had gone up the secret staircase and onto the gallery, but it had been important. I remembered vaguely the impressions: a child, a handful of stars, a battered set of Gibbon, a sense of danger, fear. Something had happened in that room long ago, and in my trance I had been trying to re-enact it. I shuddered, remembering the creaking, unsteady floorboards as the gallery seemed to pull away from the wall. If Brence hadn't appeared . . . I refused to think about it. I would not go to the library again. There were plenty of books in the small study. I would read them.

The room was empty when I entered, the fireplace cold with ashes, but there was an empty glass on the rolltop desk, and his smell. It was as though he had left his impression on the air, for I could feel him strongly as I examined the titles and selected half a dozen books. I expected him to step into the room before I was finished. He didn't. Gathering the books up in my arms, I left, relieved that I had been spared another encounter. I told myself that it was relief, but it was very like disappointment.

It continued to rain all during the week. I stayed in my room and read until my eyes were sore, and during the night I slept poorly. I kept hearing noises in the west wing. Once I awoke with a start, convinced someone had just walked down the hall past my bedroom door, but when I listened in the moonlit darkness there was no sound. Days stretched out, so long, so lonely, and my headaches were returning. I was tense without knowing why, and I was bone tired without having done anything more strenuous than turning the pages of a book.

On Saturday afternoon the house was particularly silent. Charles Danver had gone to the mill, and Brence was out, as usual. Susie had the afternoon off, and Cook was in the basement putting up preserves. I assumed Madame DuBois was in her apartment in the east wing. I was restless, unable to concentrate on the French history I was reading. The rain was a monotonous, steady patter, and I had the feeling I was alone in a deserted ship cast adrift on the ocean.

I left my room and wandered through the empty halls, aimlessly exploring the house, avoiding the east wings, on the second floor there was a ballroom with blue silk panels edged in gilt, the sky blue ceiling adorned with flaking gilt leaves. The floor was warped, the chandeliers coated with dust, the silk panels dark with moisture stains. No balls had been given here for a very long time, and yet I could almost hear music and see ghostly figures waltzing through the emptiness, colored skirts spreading, flowing like wings vivid for a split second, then nothing but motes of dust swirling in empty space. A little girl stood in that doorway, long brown curls bouncing as she tapped her foot, and she laughed, so happy, and then shadows filled the doorway, nothing else.

I wandered down a long hall. The air was fetid, the sour smell of mildew almost overwhelming. *Turn here,* the voice said, *open this door, yes, you know the way* . . . The sitting room had been so lovely with ivory walls and white fireplace and large yellow velvet sofa. There had been flowers, and pictures, yes, pictures of court ladies in flowered swings. Watteau. I remembered them distinctly. The pictures were gone. The ivory walls were damp. Dust sheets covered the furniture. I lifted one of them. Yes, yellow velvet, dingy now, splitting with age.

I had sat on this sofa beside my mother. She had read to me from a big book with brightly colored pictures, the two of us on the sofa, flowers in the pretty white vases, a fire burning cozily in the fireplace. I stood in the middle of the room, sensing so many, vague, misty memories straining to materialize, eluding me just as they were about to become clear. I felt impressions just as I had in the library, but there was no fear, only a warm, pleasant sensation. My mother's voice, soft and lilting, seemed to speak. "Jane, my little Jane" . . . No, not quite those words, but words so similar.

I stepped into the bedroom. I had rarely been in here. I couldn't remember anything about it, no fleeting impressions. The Chinese silk wallpaper was peeling. The beige and ivory canopy was moth-eaten, hanging from the frame in shreds. Dust sheets covered the furniture, as in the other room, and the chandelier had been disconnected and left on the floor in the corner, pendants yellow with age, cobwebs strung across the branches. A picture in an ornate gold frame leaned against the wall, only the back of it visible. I turned it around and knelt to examine it.

Though the canvas was cracked and covered with dust, the face stared out at me vividly, life-like. She was beautiful, her long blond hair falling in glossy curls, pink lips, merry blue eyes full of vitality and mirth as though she shared some naughty secret with the artist. She wore a low cut dress of pink velvet, and around her neck hung a spectacular necklace, a glittering web of diamonds any queen would have envied. I set the painting on the mantlepiece, leaning it against the wall, and stepped back to study it, trying to remember that face.

It was familiar, I knew it was familiar, but the wavering veil would not lift. I was convinced this woman was my mother, yet I couldn't recall that face as a living thing. Shadows gathered in my mind, thick, gray, and I seemed to hear a silvery laughter, the rustle of silk, and I could almost smell the exquisite perfume. *Remember, remember* . . . My head ached, the pulses at my temples throbbing. Through the cloudy fog I saw a faceless woman and a child. I was that child. The woman handed me a toy, something sparkling and splendid, and then there was fear, a fear that caused me to tremble now as I stood in the deserted bedroom.

A floorboard creaked. It was a very real sound, coming from the sitting room. I listened, every nerve taut, and the sound was repeated, soft, surreptitious. There was a pause. I could sense a presence in that room, pausing, listening, and the fear welled up. I clenched my hands, even more frightened than I had been on the gallery. I was alone in an abandoned part of the house. Everyone was gone. I was helpless, at the mercy of—No, you imagined the sound, I admonished. You must get hold of yourself.

Something rustled crisply. There was another soft footstep.

I whirled around to see Madame DuBois hovering in the doorway. There was a startled look on her thin face. I should have known! Cold fury replaced the fear.

"What's the meaning of this!" I exclaimed.

"I thought—"

"Why are you spying on me!"

"Really, Miss Danver—"

"Don't try to deny it. You've been spying on me ever since I arrived. Why? What do you hope to discover?"

"You're imagining things," she said.

"Am I indeed? I think not, Madame DuBois."

I had caught her in the act, yet she had the gall to deny that she had been spying. I glared at her with frigid rage, and the woman drew back a step or two. She hadn't counted on being detected. She had thought she could watch me unobserved, slipping into the shadows or behind a piece of furniture when I turned to leave the room. She was slightly flustered, but it took her only a moment to regain that haughty composure.

"Perhaps you'd better explain your presence in this part of the house, Madame DuBois," I said coldly.

"I was—"

"You were following me, weren't you?"

"Yes," she admitted. "I thought it might be a good idea."

"Why?"

"You might have gotten lost," she replied. It was a feeble excuse. Even she realized that.

"And you could show me the way back," I said.

"Yes."

"I'm afraid that's not a very satisfactory explanation," I retorted. "I don't like this, Madame. I don't like it at all."

She made no reply. Although she was as stiff and disdainful as ever, there was a worried look in her eyes. Was she actually afraid I would report this to my guardian? No. There was another explanation for that look of apprehension. She knew something that I didn't know. Something was going on, and it involved me. There was a very important reason for her spying.

"This was my mother's bedroom, wasn't it?" I said abruptly.

"How did—I wouldn't know," she replied, catching herself just in time.

"You're lying," I said.

"There are so many bedrooms. It was such a long time ago."

"The woman in the painting was my mother."

"I wouldn't know."

"My mother was French. You are French. You knew her. You must have known her."

"No," she said. "I suggest you leave this part of the house, Miss Danver. It really isn't safe. The wood is rotten. The plaster is loose. An accident could happen. You barely avoided one in the library last week. I should think it would have made you more cautious."

She left before I could make a rejoinder, hurrying across the sitting room with a loud crackle of taffeta skirts. How did she know about the incident in the library? Brence had said that he told no one, and I believed him. She must have been there all the time, watching, Brence and I both unaware of her presence. I frowned, disturbed and completely frustrated. I couldn't understand any of it, yet once again I had the distinct impression that I was the central figure in some secret drama. The other players knew the plot and the roles they must play, while I was left to wander aimlessly about the stage without the least idea what was going on.

Charles Danver was more attentive that night than he had ever been before. He made idle conversation at the dining table, asking me questions about the school, telling me about the mill and the fabrics it produced. All the while he watched me carefully, studying me. I was extremely uncomfortable, finding his previous silent indifference preferable to this. The candles flickered, casting warm shadows over the white linen cloth, reflecting on silver and crystal. I was relieved when the meal was over. It had been a great strain on my nerves.

Charles Danver accompanied me to the main hall. Ordinarily he went immediately to the drawing room, but tonight he paused, lingering beside me. He wore a dark brown suit and an orange satin vest patterned with brown and black leaves. Suit and vest were both a bit rumpled, and his brown stock was crushed. He sighed, lifting his heavy shoulders, and then he laid a hand on my shoulder. I tightened up nervously. My guardian smiled wryly, his eyes dark with amusement.

"Do you imagine I plan to throttle you?"

"Of—of course not," I stammered.

"Relax. I mean you no harm."

"Your—friendliness bewilders me."

"Do you still imagine I'm a dark arch-villian? I don't wonder. I was rather rough on you when you first arrived. I had been having difficulties at the mill, difficulties with my son. I wasn't in a pleasant frame of mind that morning."

He chuckled softly. I wasn't for a moment taken in by his pretense of amiability.

"Do you need anything, Jane?" he inquired.

"No," I said.

"No pin money? You wouldn't like a new dress?"

"I require nothing, thank you."

"You're as prickly as a cactus. That isn't admirable in a young girl. You must learn to loosen up."

He removed his hand from my shoulder and stepped back in order to observe me from a different angle. His manner was casual and relaxed, but I sensed the steely hardness behind the affable pose. An amused smile lingered on his wide mouth, and the eyes gleamed darkly. I stood stiffly, my arms folded around my waist, and Charles Danver shook his head slowly.

"You're an odd girl," he said. "I have never seen you smile. Must you be so defensive, so suspicious?"

"I'm sorry if I've displeased you in any way, Mr. Danver."

"You haven't been well. I suppose that explains it. Tell me, have you begun to remember this house?"

I shook my head.

"Not at all?" he said lightly.

"I've had vague impressions, a sense of having been here before, but nothing clear."

"I see. You've been here a short while. Perhaps your memory will return in time."

"Is it important that I remember?" I asked.

The handsome, slightly fleshy face was suddenly guarded. There was a tightness about the mouth, and the black-brown eyes were flat. I was puzzled by this abrupt change of expression. All affability was gone now. He looked at me sharply, almost angrily. It was almost as though I had been impertinent when all I had done was ask a simple question. He managed to control himself and relax, yet when he spoke his voice was studiously casual.

"I shouldn't imagine it would be of the least importance to anyone," he said. "I was merely making conversation—a difficult enough task with someone as prim and inhibited as you, my dear. I have important papers to attend to in the drawing room. I must get to them."

I went to my room. Returning from her outing, Susie had tidied up the room, turning the bedcovers back and leaving a lamp burning on the bedside table. I undressed and took down my hair, brushing it at the mirror. The rain had stopped during the evening, but water still dripped from the eaves, and the wind blew mournfully. The fire had died down. There was a slight chill in the room. I slipped a tan linen robe over my chemise, belting it tightly at the waist, and, picking up the beautifully bound French history I had taken from the study, I sat down in the chair to read.

The book was a privately printed history of the de Soissons, a noble French family actively involved in public affairs since the reign of Henry of Navarre, their private affairs even more energetic. I read for over an hour, to the point where a particularly racy de Soisson made improper suggestions to Madame de Montespan and incurred the wrath of Louis XIV. I wondered idly what such a book was doing in my adopted father's collection. Although it was entertaining enough and shed brief sidelights on history, it had obviously been commissioned by a member of the de Soisson family, for family consumption. I set it aside, something gnawing at the back of my mind.

I had the feeling there was something I should know, some connection I should make, but I was too weary to let it bother me now. Removing the robe, I turned off the lamp and climbed into bed. The wind made a forlorn serenade, sweeping over the moors and swirling about the house, and the velvety darkness was soon alleviated by flecks of moonlight that splattered through the window and made dancing silver patterns on the floor and ceiling. I was soon asleep.

I dreamed.

"She's asleep," the voice said.

I moaned, turning on the mattress, flinging my arm out.

"I wish you hadn't brought her here, Charles."

"Eleven years! Eleven years I've searched—"

"She can't remember. And even if she does, she may know nothing. It was foolish. She's only in the way."

In the way, in the way, the echoes rang, and the dream dissolved and another took its place: a child, a handful of stars, glittering, fear, panic, a low rumble, an explosion. I sat up with a start, trembling. It was three o'clock in the morning. Someone was prowling in the west wing. I could hear them moving about over the stones.

Go back to sleep, Jane, you've had a nightmare, I told myself, but I knew the noise wasn't my imagination this time, nor was it the wind. I trembled, my hands clutching the sheets, and then I got out of bed and put on my robe. It was madness. I couldn't possibly be contemplating such an insane idea, but ...

I had to know. I had to know it was not a neurosis, not an over-strained imagination. I could never sleep otherwise. I was certain someone was prowling in the west wing, and I had to investigate. That determination was even stronger than the fear that caused my whole body to shiver.

Opening the door as quietly as possible, I slipped out into the hall. It was probably Susie, I reasoned, having a clandestine meeting with Johnny Stone . . . or Brence staggering around in a drunken stupor. The hall was a nest of moving shadows, and it was cold, the wind whistling through the ruins and blowing through the opening. The skirt of my robe billowed. My loose hair spilled over my face in soft waving strands. I pushed them back and crept slowly along the hall until I reached the doorway that led into the ruined wing.

I saw a black sky sprinkled with frosty stars, broken walls silhouetted against it. My pulse was racing, and I felt sure I would collapse with fear. Perhaps I was still asleep. Perhaps this was still part of the nightmare. Stepping over stones, moving alongside half-standing walls, I entered the labyrinth of ruined rooms, jagged walls standing at crazy angles, some completely fallen, replaced by piles of stones higher than my head.

"Susie! Is that you?" I called.

The wind caught the words, shattered them.

"Brence?"

Whispers all around me, but no footsteps now, no sound but the sound of the wind and my own pounding heartbeat. There was someone here. I could sense it. Someone was watching me, waiting. I stopped, leaning against a shoulder-high wall, and then I saw the light. It was very dim, barely visible, a spot of yellow that vanished quickly, swinging out of sight. Someone carring a hooded lantern, I thought. The lights. Johnny had mentioned the lights. The villagers thought the west wing was haunted, but ghosts didn't carry swinging lanterns.

I felt as though something had called me, but I was awake now, not in a trance as I had been in the library. My conscious mind had given the directions. I listened, and there were no footsteps, no lights, only the sensation of being watched. I could almost feel the eyes touching me, and the fear was tangible, gripping me with physical force.

The ruins were splattered with moonlight. At the end of what would have been the main hall I could see a curving stone staircase climbing up into empty air, broken off abruptly, leading nowhere. Beyond it were dark caves, rooms that had retained their ceilings. The second story had been completely demolished, but part of the first remained, crumbled, shattered, buried in rubble

I stood there for perhaps ten minutes, perhaps two, time without meaning in this eerie world of rubble and ruin, and then I crept forward, frowning. I was not so frightened now. I could have been mistaken after all. I might have imagined the footsteps and the eyes watching me, a continuation of the nightmare that had awakened me. I walked toward the point where I had seen the light. Seen, or imagined I saw? What would anyone be doing in the ruins at this hour? A thief could not hope to find anything here. He would be stealthily hunting the silver in the dining room.

I stepped through a still-standing doorway and found myself in a damp, clammy cave that had once been a room. The sky was gone. The moonlight vanished. Shadows stirred, the wind soaring through the cracked walls with a sound like breathing, heavy breathing, someone leaning against the wall and breathing heavily. It was so real, so . . . I froze statue-still. It was not the wind. Someone was in the room. I could see a dark form merging into the darkness, the shape barely silhouetted against the lighter darkness behind it. I could feel the presence, the evil, and the eyes were watching me again.

A tremor went through my body. I could feel my knees grow weak.

Please wake up, I prayed. Please, please wake up.

The dark form disengaged itself from the shadows. I heard the pebbles rolling underfoot as it moved toward me. I cried out, but the sound was a tight croak. I managed to turn and stumble toward the door, and then the explosion of pain crashed against the side of my head and lights dazzled me and I went hurtling down into oblivion.

CHAPTER SEVEN

I was drifting through the blackness, floating without effort, and it was pleasant, serene and relaxing. Only on occasion did I surface, and then everything was blurred, colors melting, shapes dissolving. I was vaguely aware of Susie's face, and someone put cool cloths on my forehead. Oblivion was sweet, and I was free to drift on and on in the calm black world where no effort was required. Later, the voices began to speak, but they were fuzzy and distorted and seemed to come from a long way off.

"She was walking in her sleep. She stumbled and fell, knocked her head against a stone." It was my guardian. His voice was strained.

Later: "Charles, what if she—"

"Shut up! The maid may return at any moment."

Time passed, flowing blackly.

"She doesn't wake up, Madame. She smiles occasionally, and sometimes she looks at me, but she won't wake up—" It was Susie. "Will she be all *right?*"

"The doctor says it's merely a slight concussion."

Later, much later: "And how is she today?" The voice was brusque and businesslike.

"She sat in the chair while I changed the sheets. She drank the broth and the warm milk. She seemed to relax more after you gave her that drug."

"She's coming round. No danger. She'll have to stay in bed for several days. Complete rest. Absolute quiet."

Black waves rose and fell, slipping away, and the room was a whirl of blurry colors spinning slowly, growing steady, coming into focus. I was alone. There was a tray by the bedside and a long velvet cord hanging from the ceiling. I closed my eyes and drifted back into the serene black comfort waiting to embrace me.

Jamintha smiled. She was vague and misty, and I knew she was a dream creature, her voice in my mind. "I promised to come. I said we would be together. Don't worry, Jane. Don't worry."

Sunshine spilled into the room, bright and sparkling. I sat up with a start. My forehead was damp and clammy, and my head ached painfully. I was weary, so weary I could hardly reach for the cord and pull it. I felt as though I had been hiking over the moors for days on end without resting. I pulled the cord, and in a few moments Susie came into the room, smiling pleasantly.

"Yes, Miss Jane?" she said. She seemed perfectly normal. There was no concern in her eyes.

"What—what is today?"

"Wednesday, Ma'am. Naturally. Will you be wanting your breakfast now? Cook has made some marvelous scones, and she brought a jar of cherry marmalade up from the pantry especially for you."

"Wednesday?" I said.

"You're looking much better this morning. Doctor Green said it would take at least a week for you to get your color back."

"A week has passed?"

"A week and a half," she said brightly. "Of course, you'll have to stay in bed for a long time and build up your strength, but your fever is gone. So is the bruise."

I touched the side of my head, just above my left ear. It was tender and sore, but not really painful.

"How long was I unconscious?"

"Three days. You don't *remember?*"

"I—I wasn't sure," I said, trying to hide my bewilderment.

"It's a glorious day, isn't it?" she remarked, stepping to the window to relish the sunshine. "Oh, by the way, I gave Johnny your note. He says to tell you he's glad you're feeling so much better. It *was* thoughtful of him to send those flowers. They're beginning to wilt. I guess I'd better take them out."

On the dresser set a vase of blue and purple wildflowers, the blooms drooping sadly, a few petals scattered on the surface of the dresser. Susie took the flowers out of the vase and stepped to the door.

"I'll be getting your breakfast now, Miss Jane. Is there anything else you need?"

"No—no, that will be all," I replied.

When Susie returned, I asked her to sit with me while I ate my breakfast, and I questioned her carefully, casually, without seeming to do so. She babbled merrily, supplying vital information without being aware that she was doing so. After a while she left, taking the breakfast tray with her, and I thought about what I had learned.

I had been sleepwalking on Saturday night. I had fallen and struck my head on a stone. I was unconscious for three days, but a week ago I had revived, to all appearances completely conscious and coherent. Doctor Green had informed my guardian that I needed absolute quiet and that it might be necessary for me to rest and recuperate for several weeks. Charles Danver had had the bell cord installed in my bedroom. If I needed anything, I had merely to pull it and Susie would come. The rest of the time I would be left alone.

During the past week, I had seen the doctor twice. He was pleased with my condition, pleased with the way Susie was taking care of me. Johnny had sent flowers, and I had written him a thank you note. I had talked to Susie in a totally rational manner. I had even read a couple of books, abandoning the French history for something lighter, novels by Marie Corelli which Charles Danver had purchased at the stationer's shop in Danmoor.

The week was lost. I remembered none of it. I remembered leaving my bedroom that Saturday night, and I knew I hadn't been sleepwalking. I remembered the ruins vividly, the fear I had felt, and then everything seemed to blur. A dark form? Shadows? I dimly remembered going into the ruined room. I had heard something, something . . . beyond that my mind was blank. I didn't know what had happened, but I was convinced there was another explanation.

I was exhausted and thinking required far too much effort. I closed my eyes, eager to recapture the pleasant oblivion. It was several hours before I woke up again. The sun was going down, the bedroom filled with a golden-red light. Someone was knocking on the door. I sat up, rubbing my eyes. The knocking continued.

"Come in," I called weakly.

Charles Danver stepped into the bedroom. He carried a parcel wrapped in brown paper. He wore a brown and yellow check tweed suit and a dark yellow vest, and his handsome face was lined with fatigue. His dark eyes were grave as he looked at me, and his hair was as tousled as ever, curling thickly at the back of his neck and tumbling over his forehead. In the confined area of the room, he seemed even larger, his presence overwhelming and disturbing.

"The maid says you're much better," he remarked. His voice was heavy, solemn.

I nodded, smiling a feeble smile.

"I would have come to see you sooner. I've been very busy at the mill this past week. The men are growing slack. I have to keep an eye on them constantly if I want things to run smoothly."

Propped up against the headboard, two fluffy pillows behind my back, I looked at Charles Danver with nervous eyes. His presence here made me uncomfortable. He radiated ruddy health and strength. Weak, confined to the bed, I felt vulnerable, at the mercy of a superior force, a small woods creature closed in with a magnificent lion.

"I've brought you some more novels," he said gravely. "Did you enjoy the others?"

"Yes. It was—thoughtful of you to buy them for me."

He stepped over to place the parcel on the bedside table. He was very near now, his legs almost touching the side of the bed. I noticed the way the yellow vest stretched tightly across the slightly thickening waist, the way his large hands hung at his sides, the powerful fingers loosely cupped. The pungent leathery male odor was strong. I drew back against the pillows, gripping the sheets nervously.

"You seem uneasy," he said.

"I'm—I'm just so very tired."

"That's natural. You'll be weak for some time. Doctor Green said you were to have no visitors, but I'm breaking his rule. I wanted to see for myself that you were really progressing."

He had come for another reason. I sensed it.

"Does your head still hurt?"

"It—throbs some. I just want to sleep—"

"I won't stay long. What were you doing wandering around in the ruins, Jane?"

"I suppose I was—sleepwalking," I said carefully.

"You don't remember anything about that night?"

"I don't remember anything," I lied. "Susie said I fell down and hit my head."

He sighed deeply, his chest heaving. I couldn't be sure, but I thought a look of relief passed over his face. He straightened up and tugged at the lapels of his jacket, ready to leave now. He glanced around the room as though distracted, forgetting all about me. He walked over to the door with a preoccupied expression, opened it and then turned around.

"You won't be disturbed again," he said in a bored voice. "You must try and regain your strength. Stay in bed. Rest. Don't try to get up until you're absolutely sure you're ready."

"I won't," I promised.

"The girl will see that you have everything you need. Green says she's a fine nurse."

He left. I knew he had come because he wanted to

know if I remembered what had happened that night in the west wing. Satisfied that I didn't remember anything, he had put the matter out of his mind. Was he afraid that I might remember? Did *he* know what had happened? I frowned, my head aching painfully. Another mystery. Another suspicion. I couldn't think about it now. Later . . . later when I felt stronger.

The days that followed were peculiar. I seemed to sleep most of the time, and when I was awake I was still weary, as though I'd had no sleep at all. The headaches continued, a dull throbbing at times, at times excruciatingly painful. I felt foggy and drowsy, disconnected. My dreams were disturbing. I kept seeing a beautiful blonde woman with a strand of stars, and there was a scream, someone running and then . . . I could never remember the rest of the dream, but it left me trembling. I dreamed about Jamintha, too, vivid dreams that were sharp and clear when I was sleeping, but misty and vague when I awoke.

I saw no one but Susie, and she only came when I rang for her.

She was excited about the fair. The date was fast approaching, and she was looking forward to it with great eagerness. She had made a new dress for the occasion and insisted on modeling it for me. Her tarnished gold curls bouncing, she whirled around, holding out the skirt. The dress was dark gold muslin patterned with tiny brown and yellow flowers, worn over several yellow petticoats. It was extremely tight at the waist and the neckline was decidedly immodest, much too low.

"Wait till Johnny sees me in *this!*" she exclaimed, admiring herself in the mirror. "He won't be able to contain himself, and that's the truth. Do you think it's terribly brazen, Miss Jane?"

"Well—"

"I worked ever so hard making it."

"You look charming, Susie."

She smiled a merry smile and toyed with the full skirt. "I do wish you were able to go," she said. "I know you can't, but I'd like to see you enjoying yourself. You just stay in here all alone, sleeping so much, reading those books. Sometimes hours and hours go by and you don't ring. I worry about you, truly I do. Many's the time I've wanted to come in to check on you, but I was afraid you'd be asleep and I'd disturb you."

"That's very thoughtful of you, Susie, but I do need my rest. Doctor Green says I just require peace and quiet for a while. I'll get better."

"I'm sure you will," she said pertly. "I'll just go fetch you a glass of warm milk now, Miss. You're looking a bit peaky, and I'm sure I've worn you out with my silly chatter."

Three more days passed. I did not seem to be improving at all, and Doctor Green came again. He examined me at length, told me there was nothing to worry about and left a bottle of medicine with Susie. I took it dutifully, and it alleviated the headache considerably, although I was still extremely weak and tired. I did not wake up the next day until almost six o'clock in the afternoon. Susie was in a state when I finally rang.

"I put my ear against the door and *listened* several times," she said, "and it was so quiet! I could almost have believed the room was *empty*. You must have slept soundly, Miss Jane."

"It was probably the medicine," I replied.

"I imagine so. We've had quite an exciting day, Miss Jane. I was going about my business this morning, polishing the silver, when—"

I paid scarce attention to her prattle. I was trying to remember the dream. I had been walking through the woods beyond Danver Hall. I had been creeping stealthily down the hall. It had been so real, so vivid, but now it blurred and dissolved and I couldn't recall anything else. My head was throbbing only slightly, the ache almost completely gone, but I felt weaker than ever.

"—and I stood right there with my hands on my hips and told her, I said 'Search my room, go ahead, but if you do I'm packing immediately and that's no idle threat.' Cook was as outraged as I was. She's a love, an absolute dear, but when she gets her temper up—"

"What are you talking about, Susie?"

"Cook and I were both ready to walk out, I don't mind telling you. We work *hard*, both of us, and we both have to put up with a lot. Cook *slaves* in the kitchen, and I'm supposed to pick up after everyone and do the dusting and the polishing and the scrubbing and—well, I was simply *livid* and she knew it."

"What *hap*pened?" I said impatiently.

"Weren't you listening? Someone stole Madame's pin money—over fifty pounds, it was. She kept it in a little lacquer chest on her dresser, and when she opened it this morning the money was missing. Had a fit, she did. Claimed Cook or I had stolen it. Let me tell you, that was a mis*take!* Cook turned red as a beet when Madame demanded to search our rooms, and I told her, I said—"

"Did she search your rooms?" I interrupted.

"Not likely, she didn't. 'You open that door, Madame, and I pack up here and now,' I said, and she knew I wasn't bluffing. Mister Charles heard all the commotion and came to see what was going on. 'I'll not be called a thief!' Cook yelled, and Madame was almost hysterical herself by that time. Mister Charles had his hands full."

She patted her long golden curls, a knowing look in those dark brown eyes. "I figure *he* knows well enough who took the money," she said tartly. "Madame, too, but she wouldn't dare accuse Master Brence. 'I'll replace the money, Helene,' Mister Charles said, looking grave, and then he apologized to Cook and me and led Madame away. Cook's been in a mood all day, poor dear, cut her finger slicing carrots and burned the chocolate cake she was making especially for you. Things've been upset all around."

"I can well imagine."

I felt better the next day. I even managed to get out of bed and dress myself, but by the time I had finished I was so exhausted that I sank into the large, overstuffed chair, completely depleted. Susie scolded me, and I realized I would have to wait a while longer before attempting anything that required the least exertion. Susie put fresh sheets on the bed and helped me undress and brought me some milk and a slice of chocolate cake. Cook was much calmer now, she informed me, and Madame was her old self, haughty as ever.

"Something else puzzles me, though," she said, a slight frown creasing her brow.

"What's that?"

"You know the big wardrobe down the hall, the

one we had so much trouble getting open when we stored your trunk? Well, I keep mops and all the extras there sometimes and I hadn't had any trouble opening it since that day. I went to get my spare mop this morning and the wardrobe was locked."

"It's probably just stuck again," I said.

"No, it's locked. I tried and *tried* to open it and it wouldn't budge. Then I got a knife and ran it along the seam, thinking I could pry the door open. The bolt was in place. Someone locked it. I can't figure it out, Miss Jane. Who'd want to lock that old wardrobe?"

"You probably locked it yourself accidentally," I said. "The lock could have clicked in place the last time you closed the door."

"Maybe so," she replied, still frowning. "It's been two weeks since I stored the mop there and I hadn't needed it until this morning. Maybe I slammed the door too hard. I asked Madame for the key to the wardrobe, but she doesn't have it. I just used the old mop. Oh well, I suppose it isn't very important." She shrugged her shoulders and began to put empty dishes on the tray.

In the next few days I regained some of my strength. I began to get out of bed for short periods of time. I walked around the room. I sat up and read. The afternoons were lost. I slept from noon until well after six every day, but in the mornings and late afternoons I was awake, weary but determined to overcome it. I longed to wander over the moors. It hadn't rained for some time, and the days were sun-spangled, the air crisp and invigorating as I stood at my opened window.

On Thursday I stayed awake all day long. I felt

stronger, more rested than I had felt in some time. The preceding night I had slept soundly, for once undisturbed by nightmares. As the day wore on, I grew more and more restless. I felt confined, imprisoned, the room unbearable. The sun was just beginning to sink when I decided to take a walk. I couldn't go to the moors, but at least I could stroll in the gardens. I dressed slowly, trying not to tire myself too much, and, leaving my hair undone, I left the room.

I didn't want to go out the back way. Susie might see me, and I knew she would be outraged. If I went out by way of the main hall it was unlikely anyone would see me. Brence would be in the village, more than likely, and my guardian would be in the drawing room. Madame DuBois would be in her apartment or else in the kitchen giving instructions to Cook. I could slip out undetected and enjoy my stroll with no one being the wiser. I passed the west wing and went up the narrow flight of stairs and walked along the hallway on the second floor.

It was tiring. I had to stop once and lean against the wall, my head throbbing violently. I seemed to black out, and then the dizziness went away. It took me a long time to reach the head of the spiral staircase that led down to the main hall. Only a few minutes had passed, of course, but it seemed an hour ago that I had left my bedroom. I moved down the stairs, holding onto the smooth varnished railing. I was beginning to wonder if I should turn back when I heard the voices.

I was halfway down the staircase. Through the carved mahogany banisters I could see part of the main hall, much of the view obstructed by the curve of the staircase. Brence and his father were arguing.

Their heads and shoulders were cut off by the angle, but I saw Brence's back and legs. He wore a tan silk shirt and clinging brown trousers. His back was stiff, his legs planted wide apart. His father was standing in front of him, and they seemed on the verge of exchanging blows.

"It's out of the question!" Charles Danver cried. "You've taken leave of your senses, man!"

"You're not going to stop me!" Brence retorted, his voice trembling with rage.

"No? We'll see about that. I've tolerated a great deal, Brence. I've paid off the seamstresses and the barmaids. I've let you have your bit of fun—you're a man, a man has to unwind now and then. Your conduct has been an open scandal, but I've said nothing. Let them talk. My son's a wild young stallion, very well. I was, too, at his age. But *this*—"

"I won't listen to any more!"

"—this in*sanity* is altogether too much. Christ! I thought you knew your way around. You're acting like a naive adolescent. Have your way with her if you want, set her up in a cottage, I won't say nay, but put this stupid idea out of your head immediately. You can't *marry* the wench!"

"I intend to do just that!"

"You know nothing about her. She's a stranger. She's only been here a short time. Where did she come from? What's her background? She's no better than she should be, I'll tell you that! No respectable woman would let you pick her up the way you did. She's bound to be a—"

"Shut up!" Brence shouted.

"Not one penny will you get from me, not one *pen*ny if you pursue this wild course. Tell *her* that.

See how eager she is to marry you then."

"She's not eager! She's already *refused* me—"

"Toying with you, Son. She's toying with you!"

"I intend to persuade her. She'll say yes. She *has* to say yes! And when she does—"

"Enough of this nonsense! I forbid you to see her again!"

"Go to hell!" Brence yelled.

He stormed across the hall, flung open the front door and dashed outside, banging the door shut behind him with such impact that the windows on either side rattled violently in the frames. Charles Danver emitted a loud curse and stood with his hands clenched into tight fists. He trembled with fury, so angry he couldn't move for a moment, and then he banged his fist down on the hall table and strode briskly down the passage toward the drawing room. Another door slammed, the sound echoing through the house. An atmosphere of electric tension still crackled in the empty hall.

I stood on the staircase for a long time. So he had fallen in love at last. The man who took what he wanted and then strolled off without a backward glance had finally found someone he couldn't walk away from, and she had refused to marry him. He was suffering. The torment had been there in his voice, ringing sharp and clear with every word he spoke. I was glad. He had made me suffer. Now he was getting his own back.

I told myself that. I tried to believe it.

I went out into the gardens without being seen by anyone. I strolled in the direction of Dower House, my strength ebbing, some of the dizziness returning. The sky darkened, the last scarlet banners fading on

She made no reply. Her eyes were grave, and when she spoke, her voice was full of tender concern.

"I don't want you to worry," she said. "There are two of us now. I'm going to find out why Charles Danver brought you here. It may take a long time, it may even be dangerous, but—don't worry, Jane. I must go now. Someone might see me. No one must know—"

"Jamintha—"

"I'll be in touch with you. Dear Jane—"

She kissed me lightly on the cheek and hurried away. I saw her moving quickly through the moonlight and shadows, and then she was gone and there was nothing but the cold night air and the trembling leaves and the mournful voice of the wind as it swept over the moors.

CHAPTER EIGHT

Jamintha had promised to be in touch, yet if no one was to know of our connection, how did she intend to go about it? Most of the time, I was closed up in my room, and she couldn't openly come to visit, not if she wished to keep our friendship a secret. I was deeply disturbed, bewildered by that meeting in the moonlit gardens. Had it really happened? I had missed her so much, dreamed of her so often. Had I wanted to see her so badly that I had imagined it all, my own mind projecting her image there before me, giving her substance and voice?

My excursion into the gardens had robbed me of strength. I had to stay in bed for the next two days, too weak to get up, sleeping for hours on end and awakening as weak and drained of energy as before. On Sunday morning I felt better. Sunlight streamed into the room in radiant profusion. In the gardens a bird warbled throatily, celebrating the glory of arching blue sky and crisp, clean air. I reached for the bell cord to summon Susie, and my hand was already touching the velvet when I saw the bulky envelope on the floor in front of the door. Someone must have slipped it under the door during the night.

My name was written across the envelope, nothing else. I tore it open with trembling hands. The pages had been folded tightly together, and they sprang open like leaves, spilling onto the floor. I gathered them up and climbed back into bed, too excited for a while to even examine the pages. The handwriting was light and airy, dancing over the paper in bright blue swaths, Jamintha personified, Jamintha speaking to me in her own merry voice:

Jane,

I was in a terrible dilemma, torn with indecision. How was I going to get this letter to you? I didn't dare send it through the regular mail, of course. Someone might intercept it—I wouldn't put it past Charles Danver or that French woman, either one. I thought perhaps I would give it to your maid, but she would be bound to ask questions and secrecy is *imperative* if we are to bring this off successfully. I finally decided to sneak into the house and slide the letter under your door. It will be rather fun, an adventure, like slipping out of the dormitory and climbing over the wall to meet Billy. Anyway, that's what I plan to do, and if you find the letter in the morning you'll know I've succeeded.

How to begin? I'm not going to go into tiresome details. I've missed you dreadfully. I *worried* about you. When I received your letter, I knew I had to come, and I'm here. How I got here and so on is much too boring to relate. My first task was to find a *place*. Widow Stephens owns this snug little cottage—it's surrounded by a wild garden, on the edge of the woods between the village and Danver Hall, ideally located. I made a few inquiries and found out that the widow wanted to pay a long visit to her daughter and son-in-law who live in the next county and was quite eager to rent this place. I gave her a month's rent in advance, she turned the cottage over to me and left Danmoor immediately and *that* problem was solved.

I needed some new clothes—I brought nothing with me but the things I was wearing—so I went next to Miss Hattie's Dress Shop. Miss Hattie is a tall, bespectacled spinster, quite formidable in her black bombazine with a gold watch pinned to her bosom, but her shop is filled with perfectly glorious things, almost worthy of London. She was very suspicious of me, a stranger in town, but I told her that I was the new schoolmaster's sister and had come to get things ready for his arrival. (He's due next month sometime and *does* have a sister—Widow Stephens happened to mention it in passing.) Hattie was still dubious, but when I started picking out dresses and told her I would be paying cash for them she underwent a miraculous transformation and became all smiles, eager to help me, waiting on me as though I were a grand duchess.

I went quite mad, losing all reason as I fingered the lovely silks and soft muslins. I've never been able to resist beautiful clothes, and to be able to buy all I wanted went to my head. A glorious pink and white striped silk, a sky blue muslin printed with tiny royal blue flowers and jade green leaves, dotted swiss . . . I was in ecstasy, and as the purchases piled up Hattie became a close friend. As stiff and upright as her whalebone corset, she has one deplorable weakness—gossip! Her tongue is undoubtedly the longest and most active in all Danmoor, and I pumped her shamelessly.

I learned a great deal about Danver Hall and its inhabitants—Hattie was a veritable storehouse of information. After she had given me a complete run-down on the characters of Charles Danver, his son and his housekeeper, she mentioned the lights in the west wing and told me about the accident that happened eleven years ago. *Some* folks believe it wasn't an accident at all, she assured me, eyes wide with horror, though no one would dare come right out and say so. As she was wrapping my purchases, she mentioned you. She remembers you as a child, so pert and sassy, and now you have come back and al*ready* there's been another accident. The whole village knows that you stumbled and fell in the ruins, apparently, and Miss Hattie for one thinks it's mighty *peculiar*.

As there were far too many packages to carry, I took two boxes with me and left the rest for Miss Hattie to send to the cottage. It was after four o'clock when I left the shop, a glorious day with an invigorating tang in the air. I walked past the soot-stained buildings, fully aware that people were staring and not in the least disturbed. The skirt of my yellow silk dress blew against my legs, belling out behind, and the wind made my hair toss and tumble. I felt full of life, charged with energy, eager to start my investigations.

He stepped directly in front of me, blocking my way.

"Haven't I met you somewhere before?" he said. Those magnificent blue eyes stared at me with shattering intensity, sending a message I couldn't help but receive.

"I'm afraid not," I replied blithely.

"You look familiar—somehow I feel I've met you."

"That isn't likely," I said. "I've only just arrived in Danmoor. I'm the schoolmaster's sister, come to make things ready for him."

"You're all alone?"

"My brother will be joining me sometime next month."

"Where are you staying?"

"I don't think that need concern you, Sir. Please step aside. You're blocking my way."

He took the boxes out of my arms, completely ignoring my comment. He held them under one arm, brushing black locks from his forehead with his free hand. His eyes were like smouldering blue fire, his mouth tight. I knew immediately that he desired me, and I knew the advantage that gave me.

"I'll carry them for you," he said. His voice was husky, very low, and he expected me to melt. He *is* quite seductive, but then I'm no wide-eyed village maiden. I smiled, amused by his arrogance and his assumption that I would fall right in with his scheme.

"Very well," I said. "It's a long walk. I'm staying at Widow Stephens' cottage on the edge of town. I hope you're up to it."

As we walked along the pavement, he was silent, impatient to reach our destination. I laughed inside, knowing what he expected, knowing how disappointed he was going to be. Men like Brence Danver think they have merely to snap their fingers to have any woman they want, and it was high time he had a lesson. We walked under the oak trees, leaves making dancing shadows at our feet, and he was perspiring a little, tense, anticipating.

"Here's the cottage," I said, opening the gate. "I'll take the boxes now, Mr. Danver."

"How did you know my name?"

"I've only been here a short while, but I've already heard about you, Sir. I was *warned* about you, in fact."

"But you let me carry your packages," he said, grinning. He was all masculine charm, self-assured, confident of his conquest.

"You were very insistent," I replied.

"And now?"

"And now I'll say good-bye, Mr. Danver."

I took the boxes from him and stepped through the gate, closing it between us. He looked stunned, then angry. His face darkened, brows lowered in a scowl. He wrapped his hands around the gateposts, looking as though he wanted to throttle me.

"Did you really think it would be that easy?" I inquired lightly.

"What do you mean?"

"You know very well what I mean. Do you take me for a prostitute, or have you merely been spoiled by the wrong kind of women?"

"I thought—that look in your eye—"

"I know what you thought. You're quite mistaken."

"You're not going to ask me in?"

"That would hardly be proper, Mr. Danver."

I gave him a polite smile and went inside. Setting the boxes down on the hall table, I lifted the window curtain and peered outside. Brence was still standing at the white picket gate, his hands gripping the posts. The angry expression had been replaced by one of amazed disappointment, and he looked like a bewildered little boy who has had a shiny toy snatched out of his hands. I laughed softly and let the curtain fall back in place. Brence Danver was going to have a restless evening, and he was going to do quite a lot of thinking about the schoolmaster's sister.

He came the next afternoon with a bouquet of flowers. I refused them, and I refused to let him in. On the following day he came again, bearing another bouquet. I took the flowers, thanked him politely and closed the door on him. He looked miserable. Things were going exactly as planned. On the third day I greeted him amiably and ushered him into the small, over-crowded parlor with its brass fire screen and crocheted doilies.

"Won't you sit down, Mr. Danver," I said, gesturing toward the stiff horsehair sofa.

He sat, spreading his palms over his knees and

looking immensely uncomfortable. He wore a dark gray suit with a sapphire blue waistcoat, his white linen shirtfront ruffled. His boots were highly glossed, the black leather silvery, and his hair was neatly combed, only slightly disarrayed by the wind. I served tea and sat down across from him, an ultra-respectable young Victorian maiden entertaining a gentleman caller with perfect poise. An invisible chaperone seemed to be sitting in the parlor with us. Brence held his tea cup awkwardly, completely out of his element.

"I want to thank you again for the flowers," I said. "They're lovely."

"Uh, sure—" he muttered.

For the next half hour I engaged him in the most trivial conversation, playing my role to the hilt. The poor man was totally at sea, not knowing what to say or do. The arrogance was gone, and he was no longer confident. He wanted to flee, yet he stayed. He had to stay. In my new muslin dress I had never looked lovelier, and it was no accident. He was fascinated, as I had meant for him to be, and he endured the trivial chatter, devouring me with his eyes.

"I must ask you to leave now, Mr. Danver," I said after a while.

"I'll call on you again tomorrow."

"Wouldn't that be a waste of your time?" I asked lightly.

"I'll be here tomorrow," he said brusquely.

I've no doubt he went immediately to a pub and got roaring drunk. He had never met anyone quite like the schoolmaster's sister, and he didn't know how to react. The accomplished lady killer was gone. The wild young rakehell who plundered female hearts and rode his black stallion over the moors was as putty in my hands. He came to call the next afternoon, and the next, awkward, ill at ease, unable to stay away, and I took a certain satisfaction in tormenting him. He was sulky and irritable, yet he never got out of hand, not during those first three visits.

On the fourth afternoon he was in a thunderous mood, all the violence in his nature welling up. There was something on his mind, and he seemed about to explode. I greeted him politely and let him into the parlor. He refused to sit. He stalked about the room, for all the world like a caged panther. I poured the tea and handed it to him. He stared down at the cup and saucer in his hand and then hurled them into the fireplace. The china shattered into a dozen pieces.

"Mr. Danver!" I protested.

"Where were you last night?" His voice was low, and there was an undeniable menace in his tone.

"I—I really don't think that's any of your business."

He stared at me, his handsome face granite hard. His eyes gleamed with dark blue fury, and I could see that he was fighting to control himself. I had planned this, had deliberately brought him to this point, yet I couldn't help but feel a tremor of alarm. He is a man of tumultuous passions, ruled by those passions, caution and restraint unknown. One senses a barely repressed savagery even when he is in repose, and now that he was angry he was formidable indeed.

"I came last night," he said. "I couldn't stay away. You've driven me out of my mind—you know that! I had to see you. I pounded on the door. No one answered. I waited. For over two hours I waited! Where were you? I intend to find out!"

I didn't answer. He seized my arms, his fingers digging painfully into the flesh.

"Tell me! If there's another man—by God, if there's another man I'll kill him!"

"There is no other man, Brence."

"This game we've been playing—"

"You're hurting me. You have no right to—"

"I'm in love with you! Can't you see that!"

He released me and dropped onto the sofa, all the spirit suddenly gone out of him. He looked exhausted and abject and thoroughly miserable. Dark locks spilled over his forehead. I brushed them back and rested my palm on his cheek. He scowled and jerked his head back, refusing to look up at me. He stared at the carpet, his shoulders hunched, the corners of his mouth turned down.

"I haven't been able to sleep. I haven't been able to eat. No woman has ever done this to me before! I can't concentrate. I can't do anything but think of you. I've gone through hell this past week. I can't take much more of this. I don't *intend* to take much more of it! I don't know what you've done to me, but—" He cut himself short and looked up at me with passionate blue eyes.

"Yes?" I said quietly.

He started to say something but frowned and

shook his head, the picture of frustration. I almost felt sorry for him then. Men are really simple creatures, Jane, for all their bravado and bluster. The strongest, the boldest of them can be easily manipulated by any woman who knows how to go about it, and Brence Danver is essentially a deplorably spoiled little boy who has been accustomed to having his way all his life. Stripped of his confidence, the swagger gone, he looked forlorn and almost pathetic as he sat there on the sofa.

"You've bewitched me," he said miserably.

"Have I?"

"You did it deliberately. To punish me."

"Perhaps."

"I know I made an ass of myself that first day. I thought—there was something in your eye—"

"Perhaps there was."

"This past week—this damned parlor—"

"Have you suffered so very much?"

"Don't mock me!" he yelled.

"You expected me to act like one of your barmaids?"

"I don't know *what* I expected!"

"No?"

"Look, I'm *sorry*."

I had to smile then. I couldn't restrain myself. I stepped over to the window and peered out at the garden, savoring my victory. Brence sighed heavily and stood up. For a moment I thought that he was going to leave, and then he took my arm and turned me around to face him. He had to grope for words. What he said didn't come easily.

"I've never courted a girl. I've never made

small talk and exchanged pleasantries and paid subtle compliments. Hell, those flowers I brought you were the first flowers I ever gave anyone! I'm impatient and irresponsible and hot-tempered, and sometimes it isn't easy to control myself, but—you're going to be my girl, Jamintha."

"Am I?"

He nodded briskly, his expression stern. Men have great egos, particularly handsome men, and they must believe they have the upper hand. A woman must allow them to think so. His pride had been wounded, but he had recovered himself now, once more the masterful male. It was the only role he knew, and I let him play it.

"What are your intentions?" I asked.

"I—" He frowned, confused.

"I've already compromised myself by letting you come here. Everyone in Danmoor knows about it. Miss Hattie is appalled. When I went to the dress shop yesterday she was stiff with disapproval."

"To hell with Miss Hattie," he said sullenly.

"I'll permit you to see me in the afternoons," I told him.

"I'll see you whenever I like!"

"In the afternoons," I repeated calmly. "You will be proper and respectful. Later on, I may allow you to take me to the fair. I understand there's to be a dance. I might enjoy that."

He scowled again, wanting to argue but not quite sure enough of his position to dictate terms just yet. Brows lowered, blue eyes dark, mouth set in a firm line, he stared at me.

"There'll be no other men," he warned.

"Just you," I said pleasantly.

"Just me, and don't you forget it!"

When he left the cottage in a stormy mood, I was completely satisfied with the way things had gone. He might rage and protest and lash out, but I knew I could control him. Brence Danver is experiencing an entirely new emotion, and he's helpless before it. You may think it's wicked of me to treat him this way, Jane, but he deserves any anguish he might feel. I'm using him, true, but I can't really bring myself to feel much sympathy for a man who has so heartlessly used so many women in the past.

I've been seeing him for two weeks now. It's an open scandal in Danmoor. Respectable women shun me when I'm walking along the street, and Miss Hattie has told me to take my business elsewhere. I find it rather amusing and, yes, exciting. There's not a one of them who wouldn't secretly like to change places with me. They think I'm a brazen hussy and are certain we are having a raging illicit affair. I won't say Brence hasn't *tried* to instigate one, but so far I'm as pure as the proverbial driven snow, if somewhat shaken. He's a very exciting man, and there have been one or two occasions when . . . but I don't want to shock you, dear, prim Jane. You're probably as appalled as Miss Hattie. Just remember that I'm doing this for you.

Handling a man is an extremely delicate job, particularly when the man is as volatile and touchy as Brence Danver. The first round was mine, but I realized I would have to tread softly.

There could be no more trivial chatter over tea, no more invisible chaperone and stilted decorum. (I was as tired of the stuffy parlor as Brence was, actually, but it had served its purpose.) He is infatuated, madly infatuated, but that soon gives way to boredom or disgust if a woman doesn't play her cards just right. She needn't allow *liberties,* but there must be an air of subtle promise, an atmosphere of intimacy. She must, in short, keep him interested.

On Tuesday, I suggested a picnic in the woods beyond the cottage, and when he came on Wednesday I met him at the door with a yellow straw hamper packed with food. Brence took it, and we were soon strolling beneath the trees, limbs groaning overhead, the path carpeted with yellow and bronze and dark gold leaves that crackled underfoot. I felt glorious, intoxicated by the crisp clear air scented with autumn and the brilliant sunlight that streamed down in sparkling rays. I was carefree and blithe, attuned to woodland sounds and woodland smells and savoring them all. Brence was silent and moody, lugging the hamper under one arm and glaring at the birds who warbled so lustily at our approach.

"Where're we going?" he asked grumpily. "This thing's heavy."

"I have a spot all picked out. A beautiful clearing."

Brence groaned and shifted the hamper under his arm. Taking a childish pleasure in the outing, I laughed merrily, the sound echoing through the woods. I was wearing the yellow dress, my long chestnut curls tumbling, and I knew the exhilaration I felt gave me a radiant sparkle. Brence plodded along, angrily crushing twigs and leaves beneath his boots. Although it was cool, he was perspiring a bit and his white cambric shirt clung to his back and shoulders.

The clearing was carpeted with short brown grass, autumn leaves scattered about, and there was an ancient gray stump. Brence set the hamper down on the stump and stood back looking helpless and bored while I spread out a checked tablecloth. A cloud of white and yellow butterflies swarmed in the air, hovering like scraps of silk for a moment and then disappearing. Taking the food out, I sat down and spread my skirt. Brence stood with his hands on his thighs, frowning.

"Don't you like picnics?" I teased.

"I've never been on one before," he said gruffly.

"Not even as a boy?"

"Not even as a boy," he retorted.

He was surly and uncommunicative while we ate, leaning back against the stump with a moody look in his eyes. Brence is a terribly unhappy person, Jane, and I sensed that the source of this unhappiness goes back to his childhood. I gradually coaxed him into talking about himself—there are few things a man enjoys more—and he described a miserable, rebellious childhood and a rugged adolescence marked by one scrape after another. He talked about his father, his voice full of bitterness. I think the conflict between them goes much deeper than Brence's refusal to take any interest in the mill.

I gradually brought the conversation around to your parents' accident. He grew guarded, clearly reluctant to discuss it.

"Weren't you there the night it happened?" I asked casually.

He nodded grimly. "My father and I had come to visit Uncle George. We had been staying at Danver Hall for three weeks. That night—I was fifteen years old—I'd met a girl in the village, I'd slipped out to meet her. When I returned to the house—"

"Yes?" I prompted.

"I was walking back. I heard a rumbling noise. I saw the roof of the west wing caving in. The walls shook and vibrated and held for a moment, and then they crashed. Stones flew everywhere. There was dust and flashes of red and—" He paused, his face suddenly hard. "And then the dust settled and there was nothing but a great gaping ruin where the west wing had been."

"It must have been a dreadful sight," I said quietly. "Your aunt and uncle—"

"It took them two weeks to find the bodies under the rubble," he said in a flat voice. "No one ever understood what they were *doing* in the west wing that night. It was empty, unused. There wasn't even any furniture in the rooms."

"Was your father at the house that night?"

"He was there."

Those three words sounded ominous. I had the feeling that the fifteen-year-old boy had seen something else, something he carefully omitted from his narrative. He grew silent and uncommunicative again, picking up a stick and breaking it into tiny pieces. I saw that it would be useless to ask him any further questions at the time. A brisk wind stirred through the woods. I began to put the things back into the hamper, and Brence didn't stir. He lolled there against the stump like a sullen pasha, incredibly handsome with feathery black locks blowing across his forehead. He was still thinking about that night eleven years ago.

"I understand your cousin has come back to Danver Hall after all these years," I said lightly, folding up the tablecloth and putting it on top of the hamper.

"She's back," he said tersely.

"You don't sound pleased about it," I remarked.

"She shouldn't be there."

"No?"

"My father had no business sending for her."

"They say there's been another accident. She was supposed to have been wandering in the west wing one night and—"

"Yes, there's been another accident," he said testily, interrupting me. "I don't care to discuss it." He climbed to his feet, hurling the remains of the stick across the grass. "Let's get out of this damned place!"

I was eager to get rid of him that afternoon, eager to think about all I had learned, but he was unusually persistent, demanding to stay a little longer, hoping I wouldn't turn him out at six. I tried to be charming and light, but firm, and he exploded into a rage, protesting my heartless treatment of him. I showed him to the door and told him he need not bother to come back, knowing full well he couldn't stay away. It was then that he asked me to marry him. I laughed, unable to restrain myself, and Brence gave me a frightening look. I realized with surprise that he was dead serious and told him the idea was totally absurd. I thought he was going to hit me. He trembled with rage and shouted some more and then stormed off to the nearest pub. I imagine he got very, very drunk that night.

There is so very much more to tell, Jane, but this letter is already far too long. Meeting Brence Danver was fortunate indeed. I am more than ever convinced that something is amiss, something that stems back to that night eleven years ago. I have a scheme in mind that should bring us closer to a solution, but I shan't go into it now. Take care of yourself, dear Jane, rest, regain your strength and try not to worry. Together, we'll get to the bottom of this. I promise to write again as soon as possible.

Jamintha

I read the letter through twice. There was a dull ache at the back of my head and my hands trembled as I gathered up the pages scattered over the counterpane to put them back into the envelope. Jamintha was doing this for me. Brence meant nothing to her. She was using him to get information. Her letter had brought him to life so vividly. He was in love with her . . . I pulled the bell cord to summon Susie, feeling more wretched than I had ever been in my life.

CHAPTER NINE

Dower House was bustling with activity. A wagonload of men had come from the village and were busily putting the place in order, beating the carpets and polishing the woodwork and washing the windows until they sparkled like crystal. A gardener clipped the shrubs and trimmed the lawn and raked up leaves. Hearty sounds rang in the air. Workmen with bronzed forearms went about their tasks with jovial industry. On the following morning another wagon arrived, this one loaded with crates of books and an enormous old mahogany desk, scarred and battered. Johnny Stone was helping unload, and naturally Susie was brimful of information.

"Dower House has a new tenant," she informed me. "Mister Charles is positively *liv*id, but there's nothing he can do about it. Some doctor has taken a lease for the winter, Doctor Clark, his name is. He plans to write a book or something and thinks the isolation will be ideal. No one has met *him* yet, but a manservant came to Danmoor and made all the arrangements and paid the workmen in advance. Doctor Clark should be arriving any day now. I imagine he's terribly old and a bit eccentric. He'd *have* to be eccentric to rent a place like Dower House."

"He plans to write a book, you say?"

Susie nodded. "He isn't a *doctor* doctor, if you know what I mean. He doesn't work in a hospital or treat wounds or prescribe medicine like Doctor Green. He does research and writes lengthy reports on nervous disorders and phren—phren-something-or-other."

"Phrenology?"

"I guess that's right," Susie replied. "Johnny said that the servant told one of the workmen that Doctor Clark actually visits *as*ylums and talks to the crazy people. Gives me the shivers, the very idea."

A flock of women came in to do the lighter work at Dower House, robust types in kerchiefs and starched aprons who scrubbed and polished and waxed the furniture. Their strident voices carried across the gardens, as did the smells of beeswax and soap and lemon oil. New curtains were hung at all the windows. Plumes of smoke curled from the chimneys, and the once deserted house began to take on a new face. Susie kept me informed on the progress, but I had too many other things on my mind to be much interested in Doctor Clark's pending arrival.

Although the headaches persisted, I seemed to be regaining some of my strength, and Doctor Green believed that a little exercise in the mornings might be good for me so long as I didn't overdo it. I began to take short walks in the gardens, always returning to my room before eleven o'clock. I slept soundly during the afternoons, usually awakening around six. After a couple of hours of reading, I ate the meal brought to me on a tray and slept again until the morning sunshine came streaming into the room. I saw no one besides Susie. Charles Danver seemed to have forgotten my existence, Helene DuBois was occupied with her duties and Brence had no time to think about a sickly cousin confined to her room most of the day. I re-read Jamintha's letter almost every day and eagerly awaited another.

Saturday was fair day. Susie was in a flurry of excitement, eager to be gone. Cook had agreed to bring my lunch and dinner trays so that Susie could spend the day with Johnny. He was to pick her up at nine, and she came back to my room to model her dress again, looking a saucy and impudent hoyden with mischief in her eyes. Johnny Stone was going to have his hands full. I envied the girl her high spirits and her lively anticipation. Her bubbling gaiety and blooming health made me feel pale and listless, although I managed to hide it. Susie was a treasure, loyal, hard-working, devoted to me, and she deserved all the fun she could find.

I felt lonely and restless when she left. My hair was tightly braided, the braids arranged in a severe coronet. I was wearing a long-sleeved gray dress. In the mirror my eyes looked enormous, faint violet shadows beneath them, and the skin was stretched taut over my high cheekbones. Susie and Johnny would have a lusty, rollicking time at the fair, and Brence would be there with Jamintha. I was alone, abysmally alone, a deep depression threatening to overcome me. The walls of the room seemed to close in on me, and I felt a mounting panic.

I hated the face in the mirror. I hated plain, prim Jane Danver with her stiff mannerisms and her timidity and fears, her miserable headaches and poor health. I was just eighteen years old, but I felt eighty, overlooked by life, never to know the joyous secrets that made it worthwhile. I wanted to be pretty and blithe, like Jamintha. I wanted to go to the fair and laugh and flirt and dance. I felt trapped, doomed to be Jane for the rest of my days, dull, pale, sickly, a prisoner inside this body. These thoughts raced through my mind as I stared into the clouded glass, and the glass seemed to blur, suddenly misty. To my surprise I discovered tears in my eyes. I wiped them away irritably, scolding myself, wondering what momentary aberration had caused me to indulge in such pitiful fancies.

The bedroom was confined and stuffy, smelling of sickness, bedcovers disheveled, a bottle of medicine on the bedstand, the room of a semi-invalid. I had to get out of it before I suffocated. I had to get away from Danver Hall if only for a little while.

The moors called to me. I could no longer resist their call. Leaving the house and passing through the gardens, I hurried toward the freedom and serenity I knew awaited. The flat, barren gray-brown land comforted me, the soil itself seeming to give me strength. I watched a bird with widespread black wings circling slowly, rising higher and higher until it was no more than a speck of charred paper against a pearl gray sky stained with blue. I breathed in the smell of peat, strong, pungent, redolent of an ancient life force that had survived centuries and welcomed me now.

My earlier dejection vanished, as had my headache. I belonged here. Here I was not an outsider, an intruder, and here it didn't matter that I wasn't pretty and capricious and bright. I climbed up the long sloping hill and stood for a moment, feeling stronger than I had felt in weeks, as free as the circling bird, no longer tormented by worries and fears. The music of the waters could be heard now, a rushing, gurgling, sparkling sound that echoed through the valley of gray boulders. I walked toward those majestic stones, soon engulfed by them. I could smell moss and damp grass and the elusive, subtle fragrance of the delicate purple wildflowers that grew nowhere else.

I leaned against a mica-encrusted boulder and watched a series of tiny waterfalls splashing down the rugged face of a giant stone, the water streaming down straight at the top, breaking and dividing into two streams, then four, glittering in the sun like liquid diamonds, transparent misty spray shot with all the colors of the rainbow. Here was age-old beauty, and if that beauty could be transformed into emotion it would be the emotion I felt for Brence Danver. I thought about him, indulging myself, forgetting my resolve. Love should be like this, shimmering, glistening, rushing over the hard gray surface of life, but mine must be welled up inside, a secret stream never exposed to the sunlight. I recalled his touch, the feel of his flushed, heavy body and the sensations it had awakened in me. How surprised he would be to know that stiff, thorny Jane could feel such exquisite things. How sad that he would never know.

There was no place for melancholy here. Leaving the waterfalls behind, I followed the mossy path around the boulders, made small and insignificant by their great size. It was sad, yes, that he would never know, that I could never tell him, but it was better to have glimpsed the beauty and be denied it than never to have seen it at all. Brence Danver was a rake, irresponsible and cruel, unworthy of such love. I realized that. He would scorn it, demolish it, make a mockery of the beauty. Dammed up inside of me, kept secret, it was safe from his heartless plunder.

I thought of the anguish he was feeling, the suffering Jamintha's rejection was causing him. He had never been treated that way before, and it was infuriating and frustrating and completely maddening to a man like him. I loved him, yet I couldn't help but feel a perverse satisfaction. She was deliberately tormenting him, and I could tell from her letter that she was enjoying every minute of it. Jamintha was wise in the ways of the world. She might be attracted to him—any woman would be—but she would never permit herself to fall in love with him.

I frowned, thinking about her letter. In many ways Jamintha was hard, as merciless in matters of the heart as Brence was himself. She was bold and dashing, unconventional and defiant, caring not a jot that the women of Danmoor thought her a shameless hussy. She considered it all a grand lark and practiced her deceit without a qualm. She was a fascinating creature, beguiling and gay, but one couldn't completely approve of her. Still, she was my champion and friend, and I realized how fortunate I was to have her. She had brought color and vitality to a drab existence at the school, coming to my aid in time of need, always there, always carefree and smiling. She had come to my aid again. I might not understand her, I might not approve of some of the things she did, but I could never feel anything but gratitude and deep affection for the one person who had made my life endurable these past eleven years.

Lost in thought, really paying little attention to where I was going, I was almost upon the man before I noticed him. He was sitting on a rock beside the rushing blue-white stream. He stood up, closing the book he had been reading and slipping it into his jacket pocket. He smiled at my dismay, a warm, amiable smile.

"Oh—" I said. "I—I didn't see you."

"You were very preoccupied," he said in a quiet, melodious voice.

"I didn't expect anyone else to be here—"

"Nor did I," he replied. "You must be Jane. I'm Doctor Gavin Clark. This is an unexpected pleasure."

"You're Doctor Clark?"

"I moved into Dower House two days ago."

"How did you know who I am?"

"I was guessing," he said. "You obviously aren't Helene DuBois, and you're not a village girl. You'd have to be Jane, wouldn't you? I heard all about Danver Hall and the people who live there before I took my lease. My manservant was brimming over with gossip when he returned to London."

Doctor Gavin Clark was tall and slender, dressed in dusty brown boots and a slightly rumpled rust-brown suit. Beautifully tailored, the suit was not quite shabby, but it had seen better days, as had his emerald green waistcoat. His hair was disheveled by the wind, a rich red, silvered at the temples, and his lightly tanned face was attractively lined although he couldn't be much over thirty. His mouth was wide, the dry lips full curved and generous, and he had the warmest brown eyes I had ever seen. They were full of compassion, the eyes of a man concerned with life and dedicated to making it better.

"I understand you've been ill," he said.

I nodded. Ordinarily I would have been awkward and ill at ease, nervous at meeting a stranger so unexpectedly, but there was something about Gavin Clark that inspired confidence. He had an aura of worn, mellowed gentility that did not detract from his obvious virility. One sensed strength and purpose, an integral part of him that added character to that handsome, rather ravaged face. His warmth, his gentility were reassuring, and I responded to him immediately.

"Doctor Green told me something about your case," he added. "How are you feeling now?"

"Much better."

"Still bothered by headaches and weakness?"

"Somewhat," I replied, my voice a bit stiff.

"Forgive me. I didn't mean to pry. I'm naturally interested, being a doctor myself. Are you going back to Danver Hall now? Mind if I walk along with you? I *think* I know the way back, but I'm not entirely certain."

"I—we expected you to be older," I remarked as we followed the mossy bank of the stream.

"I feel dreadfully old at times, particularly when I think of all the things I haven't accomplished yet, all the work still undone. My field is relatively new and full of pitfalls—they're doing some important work in Vienna, but most of my colleagues think psychology is about as valid as demonic possession."

"Psychology?" I pronounced the strange word dubiously.

"That's what we call it. It's a pioneer field, and there is a lot of opposition to it, but young fellows like Freud are making remarkable breakthroughs. I'm a lightweight compared to those chaps, but if I can make even a minor contribution and help shed a ray or two of light I'll feel that I've been successful."

"I thought you were writing a book on phrenology."

He smiled again. "Phrenology's just a hobby, really. I don't put much stock in it, but it's interesting. No, my book is about nervous disorders, mental aberrations, what causes them and possible cures. That's what psychology is all about."

"It sounds very complicated," I said.

"It is, extremely so. A medical doctor works on physical symptoms, the ailments of the body. He finds out what's wrong, prescribes for it or, if necessary, operates. A great many illnesses are not physical in nature, caused not by malfunctions of the body but by malfunctions of the mind."

"Like migraine headaches?" I suggested.

"Precisely. A person suffering from migraine is in very real pain. The headache is caused by tension and stress. Once the tension and stress is removed, the headache vanishes. The mind can do peculiar things to the body. For example, a Viennese doctor wrote a paper about a fourteen-year-old blind boy—are you interested in this? I tend to get carried away."

"I find it fascinating, Doctor Clark."

"This boy was totally blind, but there was positively no physical reason why he shouldn't see as well as anyone else. The medical doctors were baffled, but Doctor Klienschmidt was intrigued. He took on the case, and after several months of daily sessions the boy recovered his sight. He was an orphan. His parents had burned to death—he had seen it happen. It was such a shock that his mind refused to acknowledge it, refused to *let* him see it, and he became blind as a result."

"How did Doctor Klien—schmidt? How did Doctor Klienschmidt make him see again?"

"He probed into the boy's mind—not with a scalpel but with carefully chosen questions. He got the boy to talk about himself and, eventually, made him acknowledge what he had seen. Once the boy faced that fact, once he admitted he *had* seen his parents burn to death, he recovered his sight almost immediately."

"And what did the medical doctors say?"

"They said Kleinschmidt was a fraud," he replied. "They said the boy had been faking his blindness all along. As I said, there's a lot of opposition—the old and established always oppose anything new."

He shook his head, sighing. Gavin Clark was an extremely appealing man with his handsome, sensitive face and that rich quiet voice. I wondered why he had never married. Perhaps he had been too dedicated to his work, I thought. He thrust his hands into the pockets of his trousers as we strolled. It seemed natural to be walking along beside him.

"What do you do at Danver Hall?" he inquired.

"I—well, I read a great deal. After the accident I've had to stay in bed most of the time. Today's the first day I've attempted coming out. The sun was so glorious—"

"The exercise should do you good," he remarked.

"What were you reading when I came up?" I asked.

"Keats, I'm afraid."

"I adore Keats."

"I have a pile of weighty tomes I *should* be reading," he said, "but I couldn't seem to concentrate on them this morning. The sun, as you say, was so glorious, and the moors seemed to call to me."

"It's strange that you should express it that way."

"Indeed? How so?"

"That's the way I felt, too. The moors seemed to call. I—something inside of me responds to them. I become a different person, stronger and not so—so timorous."

"Are you timorous, Jane?"

"I—I'm terribly shy."

"I hadn't noticed," he said casually.

"That's because—because of the way we met, I suppose. If I'd met you in a drawing room, I would have frozen. I'd have stared at the carpet and groped for words and—and been very uncomfortable."

"Why?"

"Because that's the way I am."

"But you're not that way now," he remarked. "You seem perfectly natural. Charming, in fact."

"I'm not charming," I said in a tight voice.

"No?"

"Please don't make fun of me."

"Did you think that's what I was doing?"

"I—I don't know."

"You have no confidence in yourself, Jane."

"I know my limitations, Doctor Clark. I know that I'm dull and unattractive."

"Who told you that?"

"My teachers, my classmates, everyone—"

"And you believed them?"

"I—I really don't care to discuss it," I said.

"I shan't insist," he said lightly, smiling that amiable smile.

We were silent for several minutes as we walked, but it was a comfortable silence, despite the exchange that had gone before. Gavin Clark might have been an old and very dear friend. What magic did he possess to make me feel this way? I could hardly believe I had just met him.

Across the wide, flat sweep of golden brown moor we could see Danver Hall in the distance. It seemed very small, and the worries and fears that besieged me there seemed small, too. I hated to go back, to be swallowed up by that atmosphere of mystery and tension. Here, on the sun swept land with its rich odors and wind voice and gleaming black patches, I was secure, unlike the Jane confined to her room with headaches and weary, exhausted body. I paused without being aware of it, and Gavin Clark stopped too, studying my face with concerned brown eyes.

"Is something wrong?" he asked quietly.

"Yes—no. I—I wish I didn't have to go back."

"You're not happy there?"

"I was, once. Long ago."

"Before your parents died?"

"How did you know about that?"

"It is common knowledge. I know that you were orphaned as a child and sent away to school. I know that you can't remember the first seven years of your life. I find that intriguing."

"Do you, Doctor Clark?" My voice was cool.

"I'm interested in people, Jane."

"I suppose you see me as another blind boy. My—my amnesia makes me a freak, doesn't it?"

"Don't talk that way," he said, his tone surprisingly stern.

"You know so much about me, did you know that

Charles Danver isn't my uncle? My mother had already conceived me before she met George Danver. I'm not a Danver at all."

"He told you that?"

"The morning after I arrived," I said sharply. "He wanted me to understand my position. I wish he'd never sent for me. I wish I knew why he did." I stared at the distant mansion with its ruined wing, a tight, hard feeling inside of me.

"Do you want to tell me about it, Jane?"

"Why should I?"

"Because you could use a friend."

"I have a friend," I said coldly.

"Oh?"

"I have Jamintha."

"What a beautiful name," he remarked.

"I—I shouldn't have told you about her. It's our secret—"

"You can trust me."

"I can't trust anyone," I retorted.

We continued walking toward the line of trees that separated the gardens from the edge of the moor. As we neared the house I could feel the tiny throbs begin, mounting into one dreadful ache at the back of my skull. I was weary now, a heavy languor in my bones, strength and energy ebbing with every step. We passed into the gardens, cool and shady, smelling of leaves and damp soil. The house loomed up, bleak and formidable, casting long shadows over part of the ground.

"Everyone is at the fair," I said.

"Would you like to be there?"

"I wouldn't enjoy it."

"No?"

"I don't know how to dance."

"Do you know how to laugh?" The question was softly phrased.

I didn't answer. I looked at his tanned, handsome face with its lined, sensitive features and those remarkable eyes. There was something strangely compelling about Gavin Clark. I felt he had the ability to see within, to recognize the Jane who dwelled a prisoner behind the stiff, prim facade. I was drawn to him, not as I was drawn to Brence, but as one might be drawn to an older brother or a reliable family friend.

"I—I'm sorry if I was rude back there," I said quietly.

"I was a bit presumptuous," he replied. "I had no right to pry like that."

"I'm glad we met, Doctor Clark."

"Perhaps I'll see you again."

"My guardian wouldn't approve. He's upset that you're here."

"I wonder why?"

"So do I. I wonder what he wants to hide. It's almost noon. I must go to my room. Doctor Green said I needed exercise. I imagine I'll go for a walk on the moors almost every morning. I might see you there."

"That's very likely," he said.

I went to my room, so weary I could hardly undress and climb into bed. I rang for Cook, and she seemed alarmed when I told her I wanted no lunch or dinner. She insisted on bringing a tray nevertheless, in case I changed my mind. I let her bring it, and then I informed her that I was not to be disturbed. Shaking her head, scolding gently, she left, and I sank into a deep sleep. I remember awakening sometime during the night, wearier than ever, and then it was Sunday afternoon and Susie was pounding on the door. She was even more alarmed than Cook had been, horrified that the tray was still untouched.

"You look exhausted, Miss Jane, and you just woke *up!*"

"I didn't sleep well."

"You certainly slept for a long time. And haven't eaten a bite! I'm going to fetch you an *enor*mous meal and sit here and see that you eat every bite. I'll swear, I really don't know—"

As I ate, Susie told me about the fair, describing the gaily striped tents and the merry crowd, the livestock auction and the games, the dance at night and the Japanese lanterns that swayed in the wind, casting colored shadows over the wooden dance floor.

"Johnny and I had a marvelous time," she said dreamily. "It was ever so late when he brought me home—after three in the morning. I felt positively wicked—"

"I'm glad you enjoyed it, Susie."

"Master Brence got into a terrible fight," she said. "He was with that woman who claims to be the new schoolmaster's sister. I for one don't believe a word of it. No schoolmaster's sister ever looked like *that!* Master Brence trailed after her like a lovesick dog, surly and snappish any time another man looked at her, and they *all* looked, Miss Jane. They couldn't help it. She's dazzling. I suppose a fight was inevitable."

Susie described the fight with an abundance of detail. She had obviously enjoyed every minute of it. I listened patiently, trying to show an interest I didn't feel. I was pale and drowsy, hardly able to hold my eyes open. Besides, I knew I would hear about the fight again, and from a more reliable source.

I was right.

On Monday morning there was another letter from Jamintha.

CHAPTER TEN

Jane,

I must say this is all a grand adventure. My first concern, naturally, is to solve the mystery of Danver Hall, but I must admit that I'm having a delicious time in the process. It's elating to have a handsome, explosive man head over heels in love with me. I feel terribly wicked, but that's elating, too. Poor Brence, he's going to be badly hurt. His magnificent male ego is going to be crushed, but I shan't waste any sympathy on him. Things are going wonderfully well, better than I expected, and I'm confident Charles Danver will play his part, too, exactly as planned . . . but I'm getting ahead of myself. Let me begin with Brence.

I told you he asked me to marry him the afternoon we came back in from the picnic. I laughed at him, setting a match to the fuse that caused him to explode in irate fury. He came back the next day, trying to be humble but too surly to carry it off. He wanted to know *why* I wouldn't marry him. I told him, tearing his character apart in light, quick strokes that left him, figuratively speaking, a mass of bloody shreds.

"So I'm a wastrel!" he retorted. "Very well, I drink too much, I get into brawls, and my conduct with the ladies hasn't been lily pure! I can reform. With you at my side I could become a different person."

"How would you support a wife?"

"I could work, dammit!"

"At what?"

"I don't know. I'd find something—"

"What about the textile mill?"

"That's out! I hate the place. It depresses me."

"Why?"

"Those men! The conditions they work under, the hours—they're like galley slaves, chained to the oars, rowing and sweating while my father stands over them cracking a whip, all for a measly pittance that can barely stave off starvation. It's unjust. It's inhuman. I can't stand to see men enduring those conditions—"

"Perhaps you could improve their conditions," I suggested.

"My father has total control of the mill. He's not about to let anyone interfere with the way he runs it."

"And you're afraid to try," I said.

"Forget the mill!" he thundered.

We had reached an impasse, but Brence was

not to be so easily discouraged. He tried another tactic. He pulled me into his arms and held me in a tight grip. Lids lowered sleepily over seductive blue eyes, he fastened his mouth over mine and kissed me for a long time. It was a glorious kiss, Jane, a dazzling, heady experience that caused every fiber of my being to tingle, yet when he released me I was as cool as icy water.

"Christ!" he shouted. "You're not human!"

"I'm very human, Brence, but you're not going to win me the way you win your barmaids. You can't respect me or you wouldn't have done that. I want you to leave now."

"Respect! I'm in *love* with you!"

"I don't think you know what that word means."

"What do you *want?*"

"I want a man I can look up to, a man *I* can respect."

He slammed his fist against the wall with such force that a framed picture crashed to the floor, shattering the glass. I don't think he even noticed. He glared at me with blazing blue eyes, his cheeks chalk white, and then he made another of his stormy exits, slamming the door shut behind him. It all sounds very melodramatic, I know, but Brence is a melodramatic person, living at a high pitch of emotion, bellowing and charging through life like a character in grand opera.

I had promised to let him take me to the fair. He was to come by for me at three o'clock on Saturday, and I was waiting at the cottage, quite eager, for I knew Charles Danver would be there and that I would see him at last. (And, more important, *he* would see *me*.) I had brushed my hair until it fell in glossy chestnut waves that gleamed with highlights. My dress was pink silk printed with tiny blue and lilac flowers, one I had purchased at Miss Hattie's shop and altered slightly. The bodice was form-fitting, and I had lowered the neckline two inches, low enough to be provocative without really being immodest. The full gathered skirt spread in rich silken folds over several rustling white petticoats.

Examining myself in the mirror, I was extremely satisfied with the effect. It gives a woman confidence and power to know that she is beautiful, to know that men are going to stare at her with longing. Brence presented no real problem, his moods being all too predictable, but his father was another matter altogether. I knew I would need every resource in order to deal with Charles Danver.

I was waiting on the front doorstep when Brence drove up in the gleaming black victoria, two restless dark brown horses stamping impatiently in harness. Brence climbed out of the rig and opened the white picket gate and stared at me. His eyes confirmed what the mirror had shown me. I smiled, feeling exactly like one of those fatally attractive women in fiction, and it was an exhilarating sensation.

"You like my dress?" I inquired pleasantly.

He muttered something under his breath, scowling. He liked the dress, all right, but he knew the other men were going to like it, too.

Brence is violently jealous, and he doesn't want another man to even *look*. He stared at me with lowered lids and tight mouth and I knew that the costume was a success.

"Shall we go?" I said.

"Yeah," he retorted, surly.

As he helped me into the victoria, the breeze caught up my skirts and sent them billowing, revealing my calves. Brence stared at them in agony. He wanted to sweep me up in his arms and carry me back into the cottage. He wanted to release all those pent-up passions I had aroused, but he didn't dare. I sat down on the padded black leather seat and arranged my skirts modestly. Brence swung up beside me, seized the whip and cracked it loudly, grabbing the reins as the horses started to gallop down the street at a brisk pace. I laughed, delighted with myself, delighted with the sun-spangled day and the autumn smells and the oak leaves that rustled overhead. Brence leaned forward, holding the reins tightly, his jaw thrust out. He was tense and uncomfortable. I could tell that he was dreading the fair.

"You don't seem very pleased," I remarked. "Don't you *want* to go?"

"Sure," he snapped.

"We don't have to, Brence. You can take me back to the cottage if you wish—"

"You've never been to a country fair, have you?"

"No, I haven't. That's why I've been looking forward to—"

"They can get awfully rough," he said tersely.

"Oh?"

"There's a lot of drinkin', a lot of rowdy conduct. The young people go wild, and the older folks—well, they loosen up, too. Inhibitions are put aside, sobriety forgotten. There are gypsies, and con men, peddlers with gaudy carts—"

"It sounds exciting," I said.

"It is. It attracts the wrong element. There're a lot of toughs, chaps just spoilin' for trouble. Most of the respectable folks come in the morning, transact their business and leave as soon as the children've had a ride on the carousel."

"What are you *wor*ried about, Brence?"

"I'm worried about you! That damned dress—you're a stranger. Folks might get the wrong idea."

"Men, you mean?"

"Yes," he said, "men!"

I laughed again, and Brence grew silent. I found his attitude extremely flattering. He wasn't ashamed to take me, he just didn't want to expose me to the stares of the male element of Danmoor, nor did he want me to overhear the remarks they were bound to make after liquor had loosened their tongues. I was touched. In his explosive, overwrought manner, Brence was in love with me, that love a valid emotion despite his flamboyant methods of expressing it. As we drove down the almost deserted streets of Danmoor I felt a twinge of remorse over what I intended to do to him. Genuine love, however volatile, is not that easy to dismiss.

The fairgrounds were located in a large field outside Danmoor, wooded area surrounding it on three sides. As we drove down the road I could see the gaily colored tents billowing in the breeze, the booths and the crowds of people. On one side were the livestock pens, pigs squealing, cattle stamping in hay-littered stalls, chickens and geese adding to the din, and there was a bandstand and a large wooden dance floor, men on ladders hanging Japanese lanterns on the tree limbs hanging over it. The carousel turned in a bright whirl of color, husky lads and their girl friends clinging to the poles as vividly painted wooden horses rose and fell with a jaunty rhythm, the calliope shrill and brassy.

Brence left the victoria on a crowded lot set aside for that purpose, tossing a penny to the dirty-faced boy hired to look after the horses. He took hold of my elbow and led me past the other carriages. We were soon swallowed up in the bustling, vivacious crowd. Brence glared menacingly every time someone jostled against us. His manner was protective, his grip on my elbow clearly indicating possession.

"You needn't hold my arm quite so tightly," I said. "You needn't hold it at all, in fact. I'm not a child."

He released me with some reluctance but stayed close by my side as we moved past the row of stalls, industrious merchants displaying ribbons and laces, earthernware pottery, tobacco, various foods. Giggling village girls strolled on the arms of sturdy farmboys with burly shoulders and long shaggy hair, the girls in their Sunday best, the boys in leather jerkins and coarse white linen shirts. Brence bought me a glass of lemonade, deliciously cool with chunks of ice, and he consumed two mugs of ale himself, standing close beside me and casting warning glances at the tough-looking lads who stared at me.

"Relax, Brence," I said teasingly. "I don't mind at all."

"Like to bash their heads in," he grumbled.

"You're receiving your fair share of glances," I remarked. "The girl over there—the brunette in that very red dress. She looks like she wants to scratch my eyes out."

Brence glanced at the girl. She was pretty in a coarse sort of way, her raven locks long and tangled, crimson dress clinging to an undeniably ripe figure. She stared back at Brence with dark brown eyes, her lips slightly parted. He flushed and, turning his back on her, reached for another mug of ale. The girl tossed her head and disappeared into the crowd.

"Friend of yours?" I inquired.

"Never seen her before in my life!"

I let the lie pass, amused by his discomfort. I wondered how many of these pretty, robust young creatures he had known. I wondered how many of them went to sleep at night dreaming of the handsome young master of Danver Hall, remembering his strength and the excitement of his kisses and knowing he was forever beyond their reach, no matter how close he might have been at one time or another. The social structure here in Danmoor County isn't all that far removed from the Middle Ages and *droit de seigneur,* and Brence, no doubt, takes full advantage of his position as son of the ruling lord.

"There's Miss Hattie," I said. "Over there by the cake stall. Oh my, she's staring, too."

"Let 'er stare," Brence said, finishing his ale.

"She thinks I'm a brazen hussy."

"If only she knew," he muttered.

"You've ruined my reputation, Brence Danver," I teased.

"Yes, and all to no purpose. Let's leave, Jamintha."

"*Leave?* We've only just arrived!"

"I want to be alone with you," he said. "You know why."

"Indeed I do. The answer is still no."

"One of these days—" he grumbled. "Hell, I don't know why I put up with this kind of treatment. I oughta leave you. I oughta go after that girl in red—"

"Why don't you?"

"Because you've bewitched me, damn you!"

I smiled happily and finished my lemonade. Brence had a fourth mug of ale and dug into his pocket for money. Tossing some coins on the counter, he dragged me away in a thunderous mood. I tripped along beside him, taking in all the raucous sound and brilliant color. It's glorious to feel alive, really alive, and with Brence each second is charged. Very few men have the ability to make a woman feel that way, but Brence does. Without even trying. He radiates an aggressive vitality that one can't help but find exciting. I must confess that I was enjoying every minute of the fair.

Ahead of us a group of men were testing their marksmanship, firing rifles at a series of flat wooden ducks that moved on a platform twenty feet away behind the counter. Brence paid the man, seized a rifle and took aim, blasting away with rapid fire. There was a sharp odor of carbon, puffs of smoke and a series of loud pings. I saw with amazement that he had hit every single duck. The other men stood back, applauding his feat, and Brence handed the rifle back to the man. There were drops of perspiration on his forehead.

"Bravo," I said.

"You win a prize," the proprietor said in a disgruntled voice.

"Gimme it," Brence snarled.

The proprietor moved with alacrity, seizing a gaudy doll from one of the shelves and thrusting it into Brence's hand. Brence presented it to me with a mocking flourish and led me way. He was a little the worse for ale now but not quite as tense as before. A large crowd had gathered around a semicircle of shabby, cluttered wagons festooned with dangling copper pans and mothy-looking shawls. Weird, barbaric music rose in the air, and there was the sound of stamping feet and clapping hands.

"What's that?" I inquired.

"Gypsies," he retorted. "Bunch-a thieves and cutthroats. They make all the fairs, moving from county to county, stealin' every thing they can lay hands on. I guess they're givin' one of their dances."

"Let's watch."

Sighing wearily, Brence pushed his way through the crowd. Several of the men protested as he shoved them aside none too gently. In a moment we were standing at the edge of the clearing in front of the crowd, watching the dance. It was a bizarre, colorful sight. The gypsies were evidently of Spanish descent, dressed in native costume, and the men were almost as beautiful as the women. Teeth flashed in grim tan faces, lithe, muscular bodies writhed and leaped, beads and spangles glittered. There was something primitive and rather frightening about the dance, suggestive of blood feuds and pitch black nights and daggers drawn before a roaring orange fire. The thumping music grew louder and louder as the dance reached a climax.

Brence was obviously bored. He paid little attention to the fierce gyrations of the dancers. Arms folded across his chest, brows lowered, he kept a sharp eye on the crowd, looking for pickpockets. The dances were staged to divert attention, he informed me, so that the thieves could move among the audience and lift valuables from the unwary.

As the dance ended a thin little girl with a pale, dirty face and shaggy black hair passed among the crowd, a tin cup in her hand. Most of the people ignored her, and she looked desperate. I suspected she would be beaten if she didn't collect a satisfactory amount and insisted that Brence drop a few coins in. He did so with disgust. The child looked immensely relieved. On impulse, I handed her the doll Brence had won. She peered up at me with narrowed black eyes, her tiny face suddenly hard. Clutching the doll, she hastily retreated, pausing at the corner of one of the wagons to glare at me with pure venom.

"That was a fool thing to do," Brence said, exasperated.

"The poor thing looked so unhappy."

"The 'poor thing' is a professional thief. I felt her hand slipping into my pocket while she was rattling the cup."

The crowd began to disperse as the gypsies tried to interest them in the junk jewelry and bright gewgaws displayed in their wagons. I noticed a tattered purple tent splattered with silver gilt stars, a sign announcing MADAME INEZ. The fortune-teller stood before the opened flap, her long red and blue skirt as tattered as the tent, yards of tarnished gold beads hanging over her shabby black velvet bodice. Her face was the color of mahogany, seamed and weather worn, and her black eyes were cold and disdainful as she watched the crowd moving away to other amusements.

"Come on, Brence," I insisted, "let's go visit Madame Inez."

"Hunh? You don't wanna waste your time with that foolishness."

"But I've never had my fortune told," I protested.

"Probably have our throats slit," he grumbled as I led him over to the tent.

Madame Inez saw us coming and stepped inside without a word. There was an overpowering smell of garlic and damp cloth inside the tent, and it was so dark that I could hardly see. A candle flared, blossoming into light, and I saw

Madame Inez sitting at a rickety table, her face cold and impassive. There was no crystal ball, only a series of faded cabalistic signs hanging on the walls of the tent and a pack of greasy tarot cards in front of the bored gypsy woman. I was almost sorry we'd come. She seemed to resent us, and Brence's openly disgruntled manner didn't improve matters.

"Pay first," she said in a sharp voice.

Brence gave her the money, and she motioned for me to sit down across the table from her. Coal black eyes peered into mine, and they seemed to stab and penetrate. I had the uneasy feeling that this battered old woman could actually read my mind. She pushed the tarot cards aside and reached for my hand. She held it in a tight grip and studied the palm with intense scrutiny. The candle flickered, casting frantic shadows on the billowing purple walls. Brence shifted uncomfortably behind me. Several minutes passed before Madame Inez finally looked up. There was confusion in her eyes, a puzzled frown digging a deep line between her brows.

"What is it?" I whispered, my voice trembling.

"I see nothing," she said. "I give money back."

"No—no, I want to know what you saw."

"Keep the money, old woman," Brence said irritably. "Let's *go*, Jamintha."

"What do you see?" I asked quietly.

"You come from a big city. You are in trouble."

"Oh, sure, very dramatic," Brence snapped. "And she met a tall, handsome stranger. You're lookin' at him."

Madame Inez ignored him. She stared at me with hypnotic black eyes. I felt a tremor of alarm, afraid of what she was going to say next.

"You will die, but—you will live on."

"That makes a lotta sense," Brence remarked. "Tell me, is she going to marry me?"

"You will marry another," she said in a flat voice, "but you will marry this one at the same time."

"Bigamy, eh? Sounds right cozy."

"Leave!" Madame Inez commanded.

She stood up, hands on hips, beads jangling. The mahogany face was burnished with candlelight, a fierce mask now. Brence laughed mockingly and started toward the open flap. I took a step toward Madame Inez, and the old woman drew back almost as though she were afraid of me.

"Is—is that all?" I said.

She nodded curtly, but her eyes suddenly filled with compassion. She looked weary and defeated, worn down by a life of hardship and strife. She glanced at Brence and frowned again. He sneered at her. Then Madame Inez took my hand and gripped it tightly. I could sense her alarm as that gnarled old hand crushed my fingers.

"Be careful, child," she whispered. The words were barely audible. "Be very careful!"

"Gin-soaked old fraud," Brence muttered as we strolled away from the gypsy encampment. "What'd she say to you there at the last?"

"Nothing," I replied coolly.

"Say, you're not *an*gry, are you?"

"No, Brence. Let's just forget it."

"Sure. I didn't want you to go in there in the first place."

It was growing later. Shadows were beginning to thicken, and the sky was a dark blue, deep orange smears showing in the west. I had come to the fair specifically to see Charles Danver, and all this time had passed without a sight of him. I knew that he had been one of the judges, awarding a blue ribbon to the prize livestock, and the judges' stand was located near the pens. I suggested that we go see the cattle. Brence seemed reluctant, but he agreed, holding my arm tightly as we walked across the grounds. The atmosphere had changed, frivolity and gaiety giving way to a restless tension clearly felt in the air. The calliope sounded shrill and discordant. People looked tired and irritable. Several of the men lurched around drunkenly, and we passed a rowdy group of boys shouting and stamping as two of their contemporaries rolled on the ground, slamming and pounding at each other with lusty enthusiasm.

"Can't someone stop them?" I said nervously.

"They're just feelin' their oats," Brence said matter-of-factly. "There'll be other fights before the evening's over. Happens every year . . ."

Prophetic words.

An odor of steaming manure and damp hay wafted toward us as we neared the livestock pens. Many of the pens were empty now, the cattle sold and carted away. A farmer was loading crates full of screeching chickens onto the back of a delapidated wagon, and a group of people stood admiring the bull that had won the prize ribbon, a stout, powerful beast who snorted furiously and kicked up clouds of dust with heavy front hooves. Nearby I saw the judges' stand, a white wooden structure shaped like a gazebo, deserted now as the fading rays of sunlight glowed dark red. Perhaps he had already gone back to Danver Hall, I thought, disappointed. I pretended an interest in the bull and the fat rust-red sow with her litter of squealing piglets, all the time wondering how I would arrange a meeting with Charles Danver if he didn't appear today.

I needn't have worried. He was still on the grounds, and there was no doubt that he'd noticed me. Light was fast fading, a deep blue haze in the air as Brence and I went to eat. Wooden tables with benches had been set up under the boughs of the oak trees edging the clearing, stalls selling refreshments lined up across from them. The tables were filled with chattering girls in brightly hued dresses and loud, oafish boys who openly gawked as Brence led me to an empty table, a plate of food in either hand. Robust maids in blue dresses and white aprons passed around the tables with trays of ale. Brence seized a mug, gave the girl a coin and told her to be sure and come back shortly.

"Haven't you had enough?" I inquired. He had been stopping at stalls periodically and had already consumed far too much ale.

"I can hold it," he retorted.

"You already look a bit flushed. Don't you think—"

"Look, Jamintha, don't nag me!"

A remarkably vivacious girl with tarnished gold curls and lively brown eyes was sitting at a nearby table. Her dark gold dress was printed with tiny brown and yellow flowers, and the neckline was a good inch and a half lower than my own. She stared at Brence and whispered something to her companion, a large, rough-hewn blond lad with a wide, amiable grin. Brence noticed them and frowned as the girl waved merrily.

"Another friend?" I asked.

"She's our maid," he said sullenly, "an impudent little baggage if ever there was one. If it were up to me, she'd-a been sacked a long time ago."

"Isn't she the one who looks after your cousin?"

"Yeah. I suppose she does a good enough job of that. Seems devoted to the girl, watches over her like a hen."

"It's a shame Jane can't be here tonight."

"I doubt if she'd enjoy it," he replied. "I doubt if she'd enjoy much of anything. Stiff as a poker, she is."

"That's a cruel thing to say. You really don't know her very well, do you?"

"No, and that suits me fine. Damn! Where's that girl with the ale?"

It was then that I saw Charles Danver. There could be no mistaking his identity. He stood out like a lord among peasants, his powerful presence eclipsing everyone around him. He was standing by one of the stalls, fifty feet away from our table, staring at us with glowering eyes. Brence was trying to catch the attention of one of the barmaids and didn't notice his father, but I stared back with open curiosity, making no attempt to conceal my interest. He was wearing a dark brown suit, and a gold brocade vest embroidered with darker gold and brown patterns. Even from the distance I could feel his overpowering magnetism. Across the tables our eyes met and held, and I felt a challenge, excitement stirring inside. That hard unscrupulous look made him all the more intriguing.

We stared, and those dark eyes took in everything. I knew he thought me a common adventuress who had ensnared his gullible son. That's what I wanted him to think. His mouth curled down in disapproval, yet there was that dark glow in his eyes that every woman recognizes immediately. He disapproved of me, undoubtedly, but he wanted me. Charles Danver is a man in his prime, and I doubt seriously if that skinny French woman completely satisfies him. (Don't be shocked, Jane. Even *you* know the facts of life.)

Helene DuBois came up beside him and tugged at his arm. Outlandishly dressed in apple green silk awash with lacy beige ruffles, her face painted in garish colors, she kept pulling at his arm, and he finally dropped his stare and turned to her with an angry expression. She smiled coyly, scarlet lips parted, then drew back with a hurt look when he said something sharp. Jaw thrust out angrily, he said something else, and Helene DuBois turned to stare at me, too. Her face looked rather pale under the make-up.

"At last!" Brence snarled, clanking another mug of ale down on the table. "Rotten service around here, but what can you expect. What're you lookin' at?"

"Nothing," I said. Charles Danver and his mistress had disappeared.

By the time we finished eating the sky was an ashy gray and stars were already beginning to twinkle in frosty silver clusters. Candles had been lighted and placed beneath glass globes on all the stalls, and the Japanese lanterns made soft blurs of color over the dance floor as the musicians tuned their instruments. Brence was frankly drunk now and in an unusually belligerent mood. I should have insisted that he take me home, but I had to stay. I knew I was going to see Charles Danver again. He would seek me out before the evening was over, of that I was certain.

The carousel was strung with lights that made streaks of smeared color as it turned, painted horses rising and falling rapidly, laughing young people clutching the poles. The gypsies were dancing again, a large bonfire crackling in the clearing and sending up clouds of black smoke. A band of toughs roamed the grounds, looking for trouble, and several fights broke out, brutal, raucous battles that no one seemed to take seriously. Voices were louder now, laughter shriller, a boisterous, restless mood infecting the crowd.

Although the dance had already begun, Brence and I continued to wander over the grounds. I hoped this activity and the cool night air would help sober him up. He was grim-faced and brooding, immersed in his own private thoughts, and I could sense that the least little thing would set him off. It was nearing nine o'clock when we encountered Roger Hardin.

He was standing near the carousel, eyeing the girls, but when he saw me he quickly forgot about the others. Grinning a wide, mischievous grin, he moved briskly over to us and pounded Brence on the back, making those hearty, jovial comments men always seem to make on such occasions. Brence wasn't in a matey mood. He bristled, a dangerous expression on his face.

"How've you *been*, fellow!" Hardin cried. "Haven't seen you in months! How're things at Danver Hall?"

"Hello, Hardin."

"Aren't you going to introduce me to your friend?"

"Not a chance."

"That's no way to be, fellow. I'm Roger Hardin, Ma'am. Brence and I are arch-rivals, you might say. I live in the next county, and we frequently poach on each other's territory. What's your name, luv?"

"Forget it, Roger," Brence warned.

Roger Hardin chuckled. Tall and broad shouldered, dressed in an expensively tailored blue suit and ruffled white shirt, he was quite clearly one of the landed gentry. His light brown hair was long and wavy, his broad, amiable face extremely appealing with dark, merry brown eyes and wide mouth. He undoubtedly cut a dashing figure with the ladies, and I suspected that his reputation was as wild as Brence's. He looked me over with frank appraisal, undeterred by the pugilistic stance Brence had taken.

"You did yourself proud this time, Brence old-pal. She's a stunner."

"Shove off!"

"Easy, fellow, easy. Uh—if you get tired of old Brence here, luv, just give me the word. I'll be around for the rest of the evening."

Still grinning, he sauntered off with a casual swagger as Brence muttered something under his breath. We didn't see Roger Hardin again until almost two hours later when we joined the crowd around the wooden dance floor. The music was lively, the musicians making up in enthusiasm what they lacked in ability. Oak boughs swayed, tilting the Japanese lanterns this way and that, red and blue and green shadows spilling over the couples who danced with such zest. Country boys in heavy boots stomped lustily, and pretty girls with bouncing hair and flushed cheeks swirled, colored skirts flashing. Your maid was having a grand time, the liveliest, prettiest girl on the floor. The crowd of onlookers was as exuberant as the dancers, hands clapping, feet stamping in time to the music, an occasional bawdy remark called out loudly and met with gales of hearty laughter.

Brence and I stood beneath one of the oak trees. He leaned against the rough-barked trunk, his arms folded across his chest, chin lowered, dark eyes ignoring the dancers and staring at me with fixed intensity. I glanced around the crowd, hoping to spot Charles Danver, but he was nowhere in sight. The lively polka ended and the crowd applauded. Sweat glistened on their foreheads as the musicians began to play a waltz. Couples clung together, moving with a sensuous rhythmn.

"I've been thinking," Brence said huskily.

"Have you?" I replied, paying scant attention.

"I'm a man. A man—a real man—doesn't let any woman treat him the way you've been treating me. I've had enough. I decided that tonight. Tonight you're going to say yes, you'll marry me, or else—"

"Or else?"

"We'll forget all about marriage. There are other arrangements. One way or another I intend to have you, Jamintha. Tonight. When we get back to the cottage."

"Don't talk nonsense," I retorted.

He seized my wrist in a tight grip. "Come on, we're gonna dance!" His voice was loud. People standing nearby turned to stare curiously.

"Brence!" I whispered furiously. "You're drunk, you—"

"Yes, I'm drunk! And I'm gonna dance with you!"

Lurching unsteadily, he moved toward the dance floor, dragging me along with him. When I tried to pull away, he gave my wrist a savage twist. I stumbled, almost falling. Dozens of people were watching now, nudging their neighbors, whispering and pointing. Brence clambered onto the smooth wooden floor, colliding with a waltzing couple. The boy protested angrily, and Brence pushed him aside with a rough, impatient shove. Pulling me up against him, he wrapped his arms tightly around me and began to move awkwardly in a grotesque parody of a waltz, tripping, stumbling, forcing me to match his steps. My heart was beating with a rapid palpitation, anger, fear and humiliation clashing inside.

"Brence—people are staring—"

"Let 'em stare!"

The music began to drag, the musicians playing slower and slower as they grew aware of the scene brewing on the floor. Several couples stopped dancing and moved back, exchanging irate comments. There wasn't a person in the crowd now who wasn't aware of what was happening. The music ground to a screeching halt, fiddles twanging. A tense silence hung in the air. Vivid blue eyes filled with angry confusion, Brence stopped, clinging to me to keep from falling. We were alone in the center of the dance floor, the other dancers having made a large clearing around us. The crowd beyond shuffled about and craned their necks to get a better view, low voices beginning to buzz like a swarm of bees.

Loosening his grip on me, Brence looked around with foggy eyes. "What the hell's goin' on?" His voice was thick and slurred.

"Let go of me," I hissed, trying to pull free.

It was then that Roger Hardin pushed his way through the circle of onlookers and strolled toward us. Politely, an amiable grin curving on his mouth, he tapped Brence on the shoulder.

"All right, fellow, turn her loose."

Brence tightened one arm around my waist

and with his free hand pushed Hardin away. The crowd buzzed, and I could feel their anticipation. Hardin shook his head. The grin vanished as his lips spread in a tight line and his brown eyes turned flat and hard. His hands curled into fists. Brence released me so abruptly that I almost fell. I stumbled backward, watching in alarm and amazement as fists began to fly and bone smashed against bone. Brence grunted, staggering, and Hardin moved in closer, arms swinging wide and knuckles exploding against Brence's jaw. Brence seized his arm, jerking it away from him, twisting it. A woman screamed. Loud voices filled the air as the two men crashed to the floor in a thrashing heap.

"Brence!" I cried.

A strong hand gripped my elbow, pulling me away from the scene. The dance floor was jammed with people trying to move in closer. Hardin was stretched out on the floor, Brence astride him, a murderous look in his eyes as he seized his opponent's hair and pounded his head against the hard wooden slats. There was a series of horrible thuds, and then Hardin reared up, bucking. Brence toppled over. Lusty voices shouted encouragement, people pressing closer and closer. I felt faint, my knees suddenly weak. The hand on my elbow tightened, supporting me, and I leaned back against a large, strong body, not knowing who it was, not caring.

"Granger!" a deep voice roared directly behind my ear. "Break it up! You help him, Peters. Separate them! The rest of you, clear away!"

That rumbling voice carried unmistakable authority. A tall red haired giant in a tight-fitting black suit leaped forward, thrusting people out of his way as he approached the fighters. A burly lad with shaggy brown locks was right behind him. Almost immediately, the crowd began to disperse, the circle around the panting, jabbing men growing wider and wider. Roger Hardin staggered to his feet, a dazed expression on his face, blood streaming down his cheek from a cut under his eye. He stared down at Brence and drew back his foot for a vicious kick. The redhead seized him, slinging a forearm around his throat and pulling him back. Still on his knees, Brence was startled as a pair of strong arms encircled his waist and pulled him up. Both men struggled violently, Brence trying to throw his captor off, Hardin flailing his arms wildly.

"You've done quite a job on my son. I hope you're satisfied," Charles Danver said calmly as he released my elbow and stepped around me to move toward Brence.

The dance floor was almost empty of others now. The musicians cautiously took their seats again and picked up their instruments. As Charles Danver stood in front of the four men, Brence suddenly went limp, his head nodding. The burly lad had to struggle to keep from dropping his now unconscious burden.

Charles Danver spoke to the redhead, whom I later learned was a foreman at the textile mill, the burly lad one of the workers. "See that his cut is tended to and then drive him home. I imagine you can handle him."

The redhead smiled a tight smile, getting a

firmer grip on the still struggling Hardin. "Reckon I can at that. Come, my beauty—" His voice was mocking as he led Hardin off the dance floor. People stepped aside to let them pass, and they disappeared into the surrounding shadows. Danver turned to the hulking, embarrassed-looking lad who supported a limp and drooping Brence in his muscular arms.

"Think you can get him home, Peters?"

"Y—yes, Sir. I—I imagine I can," the boy stammered.

At Danver's elbow, Helene DuBois began, "Charles, we can take him home ourselves—"

"Madame DuBois will go with you," Danver said firmly. "Brence brought the victoria. You'll no doubt locate it with the other carriages."

"Charles—" the housekeeper protested.

He gave her a cold, demolishing look. The woman almost cringed. The boy draped one of Brence's arms around his shoulder, wrapped an arm around his waist and carted him away. Helene DuBois went after them, scarlet mouth trembling at the corners. Unperturbed, Charles Danver moved across the wooden floor toward me, and the musicians had started to play again as he took my elbow and led me away. People turned aside as we passed, but I heard excited whispers among them, scandalous speculation afoot.

We walked across the fairgrounds in silence, passing the now darkened stalls. The carousel's painted horses were suspended lifelessly in the air. The gypsies' fire was a heap of smouldering embers, the wagons gone, only an empty space where the tattered purple tent had stood. His hand never left my elbow until we reached the place set aside for carriages. The lad in charge was asleep on a pile of damp hay. Loose harness jangled as horses stamped restlessly in the traces, and there was the pungent odor of horseflesh and a smell of old leather.

"Widow Stephens' cottage, isn't it?" he said calmly.

We exchanged not a word during the drive. He stopped the carriage in front of the cottage and dropped the reins in his lap, making no effort to help me down. Sighing deeply, he lifted his heavy shoulders and turned to me. His handsome, fleshy face wore a grave expression.

"My son won't be calling on you again."

"No?"

"I intend to see to that."

"And you? Will you be calling on me?"

"I'll be here Monday afternoon. Make sure you're in."

I climbed out and opened the gate. Charles Danver clicked the reins and drove away. Brence has served his purpose. He has led me to his father. My scheme has unfolded exactly as I planned, and we are closer than ever to discovering the secrets of Danver Hall. I'm looking forward to matching wits with Charles Danver. He's dangerous, but I'm not worried about that. He's male, and the male is an extremely vulnerable animal. Charles Danver is no exception.

This letter is inordinately long, but I didn't want to leave out any of the details. I want you to know exactly what is going on. I'll write again when time permits. Take care of yourself, Jane, and don't worry about anything. I have a feeling that all secrets are going to be disclosed before too much more time has passed.

          Jamintha

CHAPTER ELEVEN

Monday was a dismal day with watery gray sky, heavy clouds drifting across it and casting moving shadows over the ground. As I walked over the moors, in harmony with the day, I was not surprised to meet Gavin Clark. He wore a shabby black suit and a heavy black cloak that rose and fluttered in the wind like dark wings. His brown eyes were warm and compassionate as he came toward me and gripped both my hands in his, telling how pleased he was to see me again. I smiled, as pleased as he, and we strolled over the harsh landscape, at ease with each other, undeterred by the savage wind or the menacing threat of rain.

I took him to my secret place. It was less windy there. We sat on the mossy green bank and watched the waterfall splash into the pool in silvery sprays. I thought about Jamintha's letter which I had read upon awakening. I wondered where she was now, what she was doing. I thought about Brence, too.

Gavin Clark reached for my hand and squeezed it tightly. It seemed natural and right. I looked at that handsome, mellow face with its weary lines and those marvelous brown eyes.

"You look pensive," he said.

"Perhaps it's this place. It's so beautiful, and—I used to come here when I was a child. I can't remember, but I can feel something, an old response stirring."

He let go of my hand and drew his knees up, wrapping his arms around them. It was a boyish position, and with the disheveled red locks spilling over his forehead he looked younger, the permature silver at his temples only heightening the effect. I realized that he was only two or three years older than Brence, yet Gavin Clark had a maturity and depth of character that Brence would never attain.

"Describe that response to me," he said.

I told him about the impressions I had felt when I first came back to this place, the little girl I had seen through the veil. I also described the sensations I had had in the library and the dusty, deserted ballroom and those emotions I experienced in the abandoned sitting room with ivory walls and the dingy yellow velvet sofa. His head tilted to one side, a thoughtful expression on his face, he listened, and it seemed right to be telling him these things. I told him about the stiff cracked canvas I had found depicting the lovely blonde woman in her low cut pink dress and the glittering web of diamonds.

"I'm certain that woman was my mother," I said. "I—sometimes can almost see her, but the veils are there, concealing details in my mind. I—I know I was a happy child."

"You weren't happy at school, were you?"

"No. I was miserable. I hated it. Life was brown and gray, like the walls, like the food."

"And you were ill a large part of the time."

"I had dreadful headaches—and nightmares."

Gavin Clark looked at the pool, his lightly tanned face held in profile. I hardly knew this man, yet I felt close to him, warm and secure in his presence.

"They—the doctors said I wasn't really ill. They said I was faking it—like the blind boy. But I *was* sick. Sometimes I was so weak I could hardly move, and the headaches—"

"Your friend was there, wasn't she?"

"Jamintha? Yes. I—I couldn't have endured it without her. She was the only one who understood."

"And now she's come to Danmoor?"

I nodded. I couldn't discuss that, and Gavin Clark didn't press me with further questions. Thunder continued to rumble in the distance, and a jagged streak of lightning flashed across the sky, skeletal silver fingers ripping at the dark gray expanse. Gavin stood up, his cloak flapping, and he took my hand and helped me to my feet. We left the place and moved briskly through the valley of boulders. The rain began to fall as we started up the slope. He removed the cloak without a word and wrapped it around me. We hurried toward the distant line of trees, rain splattering all around, the brown earth soaking up the water, turning to mud. As we moved into the gardens, I stumbled. Gavin Clark caught me in his arms and supported me. His face spread in an amused smile, and I smiled, too, heedless of the rain falling so furiously.

"I've got a fire going in the study," he said. "I could brew a pot of tea—"

"Yes. I—I'd like that."

We dashed toward Dower House, his hand holding mine tightly. Both of us were laughing as we rushed inside. Gavin closed the heavy oak door and led me into the study, unwinding the cloak from my shoulders and draping it over a chair near the roaring fire. The cloak had kept me relatively dry, although my face and hair were wet. Taking me firmly by the shoulders, Gavin positioned me in front of the fire, hurried out of the room and returned a moment later with a fluffy white towel.

"You dry off. I'll be back in a few minutes."

I dried my face and hands and rubbed the towel over my hair, the tight braids still intact. Putting the towel aside, I spread my skirts out and held them in front of the crackling orange-blue flames. Protected by the heavy folds of the cloak, my dress was only slightly damp, a few dark spots around the hem. These dried quickly, the smell of steam blending with the smell of smoke. Satisfied, I turned to examine the room.

The room, like the man, was full of warmth, comfortable, unassuming. The old burnt orange velvet sofa was shabby, its cushions lumpy. The battered, ink-stained mahogany desk was littered with books and papers. Books were stacked untidily on the floor as there were far too many of them to fit into the already crowded cases that dominated one side of the room. The wallpaper was dull tan, patterned with ugly brown and gold sunflowers, and the long draperies that framed the windows were of ancient brown velvet, held back with tarnished gold cord. There was a brown leather chair, a low table with pipe rack and dark orange earthenware canister. Dried goldenrod filled a large black and beige

Chinese vase in one corner. Friendly and snug, the room was made even cozier by the rain that pelted on the roof and blew in splattering gusts against the windows.

Bearing a tray with a squat blue tea pot and matching cups, Gavin came back a few minutes later. He had changed into old brown trousers and a once elegant maroon velvet smoking jacket with quilted black satin lapels, the garment now deplorably shabby. Hair still damp, he set the tray down and smiled at me. I was suddenly aware of the compromising situation I was in. I hadn't thought twice about his invitation. I had come because I wanted to, yet I now realized that my being here was highly unconventional. My guardian would be livid if he knew.

Gavin seemed to read my thoughts. "I'll not seduce you, lass," he said in a teasing voice.

"Of—of course you won't."

"You don't sound terribly convinced. Relax, Jane. You look nervous as a cat in a kennel."

"I shouldn't have come. It was an impulsive thing to do."

He poured tea into the cups. "Sugar? . . . No? I've no cream to offer, no lemon either, I'm afraid. Why? Why shouldn't you have come?"

"This isn't—altogether proper, Doctor Clark."

"Please call me Gavin. We're friends. You're very proper, aren't you, Jane?"

"I suppose I am."

"Unlike Jamintha," he remarked.

"How—how do you know?"

"I guessed. Conventions are grand. I'm all for them, as long as they're not carried to preposterous extremes. There's something wrong with a society that believes a man and a woman can't be alone together without immediately leaping into bed. Sorry. Did I shock you? You blush most becomingly."

"Thank you," I said feebly.

"With your cheeks pink like that you're pretty enough to seduce, I assure you. Incidentally, why do you wear your hair in such a severe style? I should think you'd let it fall in natural waves."

"I—I've always worn it this way."

"Here, take your tea. Curl up on that sofa. The fire's nice, isn't it? Glorious smell, smoke. There. Are you comfortable? Do you realize you're my first guest at Dower House? I feel honored."

Gavin Clark sat down in the cracked brown leather chair, making small trivial remarks to lull me into a sense of ease. My nervousness vanished after a few minutes and we were close again, friends, completely at ease as we had been on the moors. Gavin talked about the book he was writing, describing the tremendous amount of preliminary work that had already gone into it. He was a marvelous talker, his smooth voice rich and expressive. Gradually, the conversation shifted to Danmoor and Danver Hall, and I found myself telling him about the things that had happened to me since I arrived, carefully eliminating any mention of Brence or Jamintha.

He was extremely curious about my "accident," his expression grave as he questioned me.

"You think someone was in the ruins?"

"I—I can't be sure. I know I wasn't sleepwalking, although—although there *was* a nightmare quality about it, the moonlight, the shadows, the wind. Maybe I imagined that dark form—"

"You believe someone struck you with a rock?"

"I—no, of course not. I *must* have fallen."

Gavin got up and stepped behind the sofa, reaching down to place his hand over my temple where the bruise had been. His fingers were strong and gentle as they probed. He narrowed his eyes and frowned slightly, moving over to stand in front of the fireplace. He rested his elbow on the mantle, a preoccupied look in his eyes. Several long minutes passed.

"You still feel weak?" he inquired.

"Not—not as much as I did at first. In the evening, before I go to bed—I always seem to be weary then. I sleep every afternoon. I *shouldn't* wake up feeling tired, should I?"

"It's not so unusual," he said evasively. "You have headaches then, too, don't you?"

I nodded, toying with the empty blue teacup.

"Do you dream frequently, Jane?"

"Most of the time," I said uneasily. "Is that bad?"

Gavin smiled reassuringly and thrust his hands into the pockets of the shabby maroon smoking jacket, his back to the fire, his legs spread apart. "I dream most of the time myself." He added humorously, "and some of them are dillies. You see, our subconscious takes over when we're asleep."

"Our—subconscious?"

"The thoughts we don't consciously think, they form our subconscious. Sub—below the surface. Visualize the mind as a pond. The things that occupy us normally are like the goldfish you see swimming near the top, but down below there are other fish, to employ the same metaphor, and they remain out of sight, hidden in the depths. Sometimes, when we're asleep, they surface—things we've willingly forgotten, things we'd rather not examine too closely."

"I—think I understand."

He shrugged his shoulders, another smile playing on his lips. "Forgive me for sounding professional. Tell me about your friend. When did she first arrive?"

"After the accident. I seem to have written her a letter during—during that week I can't recall. I wrote a note to Susie's boy friend, too, thanking him for flowers he'd sent, although I don't remember writing that either. That week is a total blank."

"Not an unusual phenomenon," he said. "It frequently happens after a concussion. And you *did* have a concussion, however slight. So you wrote to Jamintha. I assume she was still at the school."

"Yes—"

I wondered why he was so curious about her. He'd mentioned her three times already this morning. In a village as small as Danmoor, gossip took the place of a daily newspaper, and if he'd gone into the village for anything he was bound to have heard of her and her "affair" with Brence. Perhaps he had even seen her. No doubt his interest was the normal interest of the male intrigued by a beautiful woman.

"She sounds like a fascinating creature," he remarked.

"She is. She's everything I'm not: beautiful, gay, lighthearted. She's strong, and wise. She's not afraid of anything—" I broke off, frowning. I hadn't meant to talk about any of these things with him. The words seemed to have come to my lips unbidden.

I stood up, brushing my skirt. "I—I must go now. It's almost eleven. Thank you for the tea, Doctor Cl—Gavin."

"The pleasure has been all mine," he said, escorting me to the front door. "I hope to see you again, Jane. Tomorrow, perhaps. Perhaps we'll meet on the moors again."

I did see him the next morning, and the next. With Gavin Clark I was a different person, not so stiff, not so thorny. He seemed to bring out qualities in me I had never known were there. I was almost natural, almost warm and friendly, responding to him as I had never responded to anyone else. We had long talks as we strolled over the land, and the talks always made me feel better. He told me about his life, his work, his ambitions, yet somehow the conversation always seemed to work around to me. He made me feel . . . worthy, and interesting. With Gavin I forgot that I was plain and dull.

When I returned to the house Wednesday at noon, I was unusually weary, my bones aching. Every step I took required an effort. I had lunch on a tray in my room, and Susie sat with me, alarmed by my pallor and the deep smudges of fatigue under my eyes. She hemmed and hawed and clucked, insisting I eat every bite, and lectured me severely, her bossy, scolding manner revealing a genuine concern that I found touching. I told her I intended to stay in bed for the rest of the day and would not want to be disturbed at dinner time. Rest and sleep were more important than food, and she was not to bring a tray unless I rang for her. After making sure that I was snugly tucked in bed, she left.

Almost immediately, I sank into layers of unconsciousness, relaxing, aches and weariness vanishing as I drifted into sleep. I slept all afternoon, all evening, and it was sometime during the early morning hours that the nightmare began.

It was foggy, but the fog was brown, swirling, and the woman with long blonde hair came into my bedroom, the bedroom I had occupied as a child. As the fog grew thinner and parted I could see the gaily striped wallpaper and the dolls sitting helter-skelter on top of the bureau. Rubbing my knuckles over sleepy eyes, I sat up and smiled at my mother, but the smile vanished when I saw the terror in her eyes. She had a handful of stars, stars spilling through her fingers. Her lips moved and she was saying something urgent, but I couldn't understand the words, just the urgency. Then the brown fog swallowed her up and I was climbing, climbing, my heart pounding against my ribs, my throat tight and dry, and there was a single sharp retort—a gunshot?—and rushing footsteps. Fog billowed, thicker now, so thick I could barely see the figures struggling. I screamed, throwing my arms out, and my throat was still dry and my heart still pounding, but I was in the right bedroom now and moonlight streamed through the window in wavering rays. I closed my eyes, sinking back against the pillows.

Susie noticed the bruises first thing Thursday morning.

"Lands sake, Miss Jane! What happened to your arms?"

"I—they feel sore. My jaw feels sore, too."

About three inches above the elbow on either arm there were dark brown bruises, slightly purple about the edges. The flesh was tender, painful to the touch, and although there was no bruise on my face the right side of my jaw felt as though I'd knocked it against the wardrobe. Susie's face was full of alarm, a nervous, apprehensive look in her eyes, and I knew she suspected that I had been "sleepwalking" again. Stepping gingerly over to the bed, she examined my arms, and then she noticed the heap of shattered glass on the floor. The bedside lamp had been knocked over, the green glass hurricane globe demolished.

"I—I had a nightmare," I said.

I remembered it then. I remembered waking with a start and flinging my arms out. The headboard of my bed was solid oak, heavily carved, and I realized that I must have slammed my arms back against it, probably hitting them against the projecting carvings and knocking the lamp over at the same time. I explained this to Susie, but she still looked dubious and began to fret when I climbed out of bed.

"Now be *sensible*, Miss Jane! You've no business being up. You need a nice long nap."

"I just woke up, and I feel glorious. My arms hurt a little, but not enough to justify staying in bed. The bruises will go away and so will the ache. I'm full of energy this morning."

"It's *pouring* down rain. Can't you hear it? You won't be able to meet Doctor Clark anyway, so—" She paused, realizing what she had said.

"So you know?" I remarked, taking out a long sleeved green dress and slipping into it.

"Yes," Susie admitted. Her voice was hushed and low, the voice of a conspirator. "But no one else does," she hastily added. "Madame's been sulky lately, taking to her room most of the day, so *she* hasn't seen the two of you coming back. Mister Charles has been at the mill every day, and Master Brence *sleeps* all morning long. I haven't told anyone, Miss Jane. Your secret's safe with me."

I adjusted the folds of the dress and smoothed the skirt down over my petticoats, smiling to myself. Susie obviously imagined a clandestine romance, and it was plain to see that her opinion of me had been elevated. My "secret" gave me a certain glamor in her eyes. Finished dressing, I sat at the mirror and began to braid my hair. Susie was gathering up the pieces of glass and dropping them into the wastepaper basket.

"The lamp itself is undamaged," she remarked, "but I'll have to get a new globe. There're some down in the basement, I think, though I won't be able to go down there this morning. Cook 'n I are cleaning out the pantry, and that's a *job!*"

"I'll fetch the globe," I told her as I coiled the braids in a coronet and fastened them with pins.

"I *wish* you'd stay in bed."

"I told you, I feel perfectly all right. It was just a nightmare, Susie. I hit my arms against the headboard. I'll just eat this lovely breakfast you've brought up and then go down to the basement. I've never been down there. I'll enjoy exploring a bit."

"You'll find the globes on one of the shelves." Her tone was weary and resigned. Stepping over to the door, she opened it and then hesitated for a moment. "I—I'm sorry I let on about Doctor Clark, Miss Jane. I didn't mean for you to know I knew, but, well, I think it's *smash*ing."

Susie left, and I ate my breakfast, amused at her assumption that I was having a romance with Gavin. It suited me to let her think so. It was flattering that she thought a man as handsome and eligible as Doctor Clark could be interested in me, all things considered. It was preposterous, of course, but Susie thrived on such nonsense and it would be impossible for anyone of her nature to believe friendship—pure and simple friendship—could exist between two people of the opposite sex.

The basement was dim, filled with deep gray shadows, the corners black and impenetrable, and as I moved slowly down the curving stone staircase I was glad I had had the foresight to bring a lamp. Fetid air scurried up to meet me, and in the flickering yellow-orange glow of the lamp I could see damp brown walls and cobwebs that billowed to and fro. The room was very large, as large as the ballroom, filled with discarded furniture and piles of boxes, an odor of dust and mildew and yellowing paper filling the air. Tall wooden shelves loomed up on one side. I saw the globes immediately, several of them of varying shapes and sizes, but all of a sudden I was no longer interested in them.

It had come over me abruptly, this feeling, a trance-like numbness setting in. There was no fear, no sense of alarm, but I could feel a curious transformation. At one moment I had been looking around the basement with interest, noting the details, and at the next I was standing stock still, the lamp held aloft, waiting for the summons I knew would come. I heard the voice, faint at first, then louder, giving me directions. I knew it came from inside my head, yet it seemed to have a separate entity. *Over there, behind those barrels, you remember* . . . Slowly, brow creased in a deep frown, I walked across the room and stepped around the enormous wooden barrels that, I knew, contained dishes packed in sawdust. There was a wide space between them and the wall.

I ran my hand over the wall, fingers rubbing the damp stone, and then I located the tiny lever and pulled it down. Creaking loudly, a portion of the wall swung open, revealing a narrow passageway. *You used to play here, Jane. Remember? Go on. Don't be afraid* . . . Holding the lamp firmly, I stepped into the passage and began to follow it. The gray brick walls were stained brown with moisture, damp green fungus growing between the cracks, and they pressed close on either side, no more than three and a half feet from wall to wall. The ceiling was low, the floor hard-packed earth as smooth as stone. Beneath its glass globe the lamp's flame flickered, hurling bizarre shadows against the walls, and my footsteps echoed loudly, the sound ringing up and down the passage.

Ahead, a soft white mist seemed to billow, growing thinner, and I could see the little girl in a frilly pink dress. Her long brown curls were bouncing as she skipped along, and she was laughing merrily, turning back to taunt someone who was pursuing her. I saw the plump-faced governess with the harassed eyes and disheveled gray hair, scurrying along, trying to catch her ward. The little girl turned around and made a face, and then the mist evaporated and they were both gone and there was nothing but damp, shadowy walls and the reverberating echoes of my footsteps.

Miss Perkins. Nanny Perkins. She was a dear, actually, grumpy sometimes and always fussy, but a dear. She read fairy tales to me every night before I went to bed, and when I was extraordinarily naughty and my parents sent me up to my room without supper she smuggled food up to me. I remembered her taking a chicken leg out of her apron pocket, her blue eyes disapproving, her lips pursed as she pulled cookies out of another pocket. She had been with me until I was six and a half years old, leaving just a few months before the accident . . . The memory vanished, evaporating like the mist.

The passage seemed to be curving to the left, and when I looked back I could no longer see the door. On and on I went, unable to stop, unable to turn back. Five minutes passed, ten, and then I felt the cold draft. My petticoats began to billow. Far away I could hear a loud staccato drumming. It took me a moment to realize it was the sound of falling rain magnified and distorted by the peculiar acoustics of the place. There would be shrubberies, I knew, and tall trees, one of them with a low hanging branch that almost touched the ground.

I was right. There was no door at this end of the passage, merely a rough opening concealed by the shrubbery growing in front of it. Through the dark green leaves dripping with rain, I could see the tree with the low hanging branch. I knew these were the woods beyond Danver Hall, between the house and the village, probably somewhere near the place where Brence and Jamintha had had their picnic. The first Danver had been a Cavalier, a passionate Royalist, and he had had the passage built during the rise of Cromwell in order to have a safe exit in case the Roundheads stormed the house. Nanny Perkins had explained that to me once long, long ago, and I had been fascinated by the passage and loved to play in it even though I had been forbidden to do so.

I turned back, haunted by those few, sketchy memories, my head beginning to ache as I strained to remember more. I walked slowly, the drumming of rain growing distant as I drew nearer the basement.

When I reached the basement, I pushed the door shut, listening for the click that told me it was securely fastened. When it was closed, one would have to look closely to know it was there, so artfully had it been fashioned.

I moved around the barrels, smelling stale sawdust, then took one of the globes from the shelf across the room and left the basement. I felt a curious calm, but there was something cold and hard inside. The memories were returning, little by little, and I had a feeling that soon the last veil would lift and I would remember everything. In my room, I stared out at the rain, and I thought about the nightmare that had caused me to awaken with such agonizing terror. It had not been a dream. Not really. I knew that now. It had been a memory . . . a memory that was coming closer and closer to the surface.

CHAPTER TWELVE

On Friday morning the sky was a faint wet blue, and although rain still dripped from the eaves and the trees outside, it no longer fell. The moors would be impossible for walking, I knew, but I was far too tense and restless to stay in my room. After Susie left with the breakfast tray I pulled a cloak over my shoulders and slipped out the back door, the smell of wet earth and crushed rose petals filling the air as I crossed the gardens and hurried along the mud-splattered path to Dower House.

It was several minutes before Gavin opened the door. He blinked sleepily and ran a hand through his hair. Wearing tight, faded brown trousers and a wrinkled white linen shirt opened at the throat, the sleeves rolled up to his elbows, he had that foggy, slightly dazed look of someone who has just awakened. He shook his head as though to clear it, smiled a fuzzy smile and, without a word, led me into the study. Balls of wadded up paper littered the floor all around the desk. The cushions of the sofa were crushed and deeply dented, and a brown blanket had slid down to the floor in front of it.

"Coffee," he mumbled. "That's what I need—"

"Did I awaken you?"

"Be back—make yourself comfortable—"

He stumbled out of the room. Feeling warm and strangely at home, I folded up the old brown blanket and smoothed down the cushions of the sofa, caressing the worn velvet nap. I gathered up the wads of paper and tossed them into the fireplace where they exploded into tiny puffs of flame and immediately disintegrated into charred black flakes. I was examining the papers on his desk when Gavin returned. He carried a tray with a fat green pot and cups that rattled loudly as he set it down on a corner of the desk. I smelled the delicious aroma of freshly brewed coffee. His rich red locks were damp now and neatly combed. Although he wore the same rumpled clothes, his eyes were alert and wide awake, and the smile he smiled was far more convincing than the first had been.

"I *did* awaken you," I said.

"Afraid so, but it was high time I got up."

"When did you go to sleep last night?"

"No idea. I worked on the book until I couldn't hold my eyes open any longer, and then I just collapsed on the sofa, too tired to grope my way up to the bedroom. I hope you'll forgive my somewhat groggy welcome."

"I wanted to see you. I knew the moors would be impossible, so—I just came over here."

"My, my," he teased, "you *are* getting brazen, aren't you? I believe you actually trust me."

"I do," I replied.

"I find that flattering, Jane. You'll have coffee?"

"I just finished breakfast a short while ago. I had a cup of tea, but the coffee smells wonderful—"

"I brew a wicked pot of coffee. Strong and tasty. Here—" He poured a cupful and handed it to me. Leaning casually back against the desk, his cup of coffee in his hand, Gavin smiled again, genuinely pleased to see me. I sat down in the brown leather chair and took a sip of the coffee.

"Susie knows about us," I said.

"Susie?"

"The maid. She thinks we're having an illicit romance. She thinks it's smashing."

He chuckled. "Susie sounds like a delightful minx. Tell me, Jane, you said you wanted to see me—was there some special reason?"

I set my coffee cup aside. "Yes. I—I don't know whether or not I should tell you about it—"

"You can tell me anything, Jane. You know that."

His voice was serious, all cheerful banter behind us now. I looked into those dark brown eyes, and confidence rose inside of me. I knew what he said was true. I could tell Gavin Clark anything. I trusted him completely, and he would never betray that trust.

"I had a nightmare Wednesday night. It was—rather unnerving."

"Describe it to me."

Thrusting his hands deep into the pockets of his trousers, he strolled over to the window and gazed out at the gardens as I began to talk. A mote-filled ray of sunlight streamed through the window, burnishing his hair a deep copper hue, etching light shadows over his face. I spoke haltingly, describing the brown fog, my mother, the handful of stars, the sensation of climbing and the figures struggling in the thickening fog. I told him about awakening with tight throat and pounding heart. When I mentioned the bruises he turned around sharply.

"You bruised yourself?"

"I—I remember flinging my arms out. The headboard of my bed is heavy oak, ornately carved with projecting knobs. I must have slammed my arms back against the carvings—"

"Do you mind if I examine the bruises?"

"No—" I said hesitantly. "I—I'll have to unfasten my dress. These sleeves are too tight to push up."

"Very well." His voice was casual.

I unfastened the back of my dress and lowered the bodice, slipping the sleeves down until the bruises were uncovered. The bodice of my petticoat was cut extremely low, my shoulders and half of my bosom completely bare, but Gavin was totally unperturbed, paying attention to nothing but the bruises. Bending down over me, he touched them with delicate fingertips, an intent look in his eyes. A frown wrinkled his brow, and he pressed his lips in a tight line, studying the bruises. They were lighter now, a yellowish tan, light blue around the edges. Gavin nodded and stepped back, his expression composed and professional.

"Do they still hurt?"

"Not at all."

"Tell me again how you think you obtained them."

I did so, pulling up the bodice of my dress and refastening the hooks in back.

"Sounds logical enough," he said lightly.

"You—you don't believe me, do you? You think I was sleepwalking."

"No, Jane. I don't think that. I—it probably happened just as you say it did. Nightmares can be very vivid, and when we pull out of them our reflexes can be violent."

"*This* one was vivid," I said crisply. "I don't think it was a nightmare. I think it was a memory. You told me about the subconscious. I—I think I actually saw those things and forced myself to forget them, forced them deep down into that pool you described."

"That's entirely possible."

"I've remembered something else, too. My governess. Her name was Miss Perkins. I saw her quite clearly, and I remembered how she used to bring food to me when I was being punished for misdeeds."

I described the peculiar, trance-like sensation I had felt in the basement and how I had moved directly to the secret door. My voice wavering, I told him about the softly diffused mist and the little girl in pink and all the impressions that had come to mind. Gavin perched on the corner of the desk, rubbing his jaw thoughtfully with his right hand. His dark brown eyes seemed preoccupied, staring across the room without seeing anything, yet I could tell that he was paying close attention to every word I said.

"You found a secret passage," he remarked quietly, more to himself than for my benefit. "Interesting—"

"Gavin, will my memory return? Completely?"

"There's no doubt about it," he replied. "It's beginning to come back already. Gradually, through association, you'll remember more and more. It's merely a matter of time."

"I'll remember—everything?"

"I'm sure of it."

When I made no reply, he looked up at me. "You don't seem too pleased with the idea," he commented.

"I find it rather frightening."

"Why?"

"I don't know. I just—" I broke off and stared down at the hands in my lap as though they were curiosities I had never seen before.

"Why should you be afraid, Jane? Because you think someone hit you in the ruins that night?"

"Partly."

"Perhaps you'd like to tell me about it."

"It will sound silly—hysterical. You'll think I'm mad, but—something is going on at Danver Hall. Something is wrong. I sense it. I can feel it in the air. It—it began the day I arrived. I couldn't understand why my guardian sent for me. He certainly has no affection for me. He's not a charitable man, yet there had to be a reason why he had gone to all that trouble and expense. *Why* should I be at Danver Hall? I asked myself that question repeatedly, and there was no logical answer. I—I soon became aware that Madame DuBois was spying on me. I had the feeling she was watching every move I made, waiting for me to *do* something—"

"Go on."

"I think Charles Danver brought me here because he *wants* me to remember—he questioned me about my memory, seemed anxious to know if I had begun to recall anything. I know it sounds far-fetched, but I have the feeling I know something very important to him, only I've forgotten—"

"And he hoped bringing you to Danver Hall would

jog your memory? Is that what you believe?"

"Yes."

"Then why should he wait eleven years to do so?"

"I—I don't know. Perhaps he thought he could discover whatever it is on his own. Perhaps he's spent all this time searching and—and I was a last resort."

"That doesn't make too much sense, Jane, does it?"

"No," I admitted miserably. "*Do* you think I'm mad, Gavin?"

Gavin Clark shook his head. When he spoke, his voice was filled with tender compassion. "You show all the signs of what we call a persecution complex, Jane—intrigue centered around you, someone spying—but no, I don't think you're mad. You've dramatized things a bit, perhaps, and put sinister interpretations on a situation that may be and probably is totally innocent, but you've been under a great deal of stress, and that concussion you received—" He left the sentence hanging in the air, making a futile gesture with his hand.

"I see."

"Tell me about Jamintha," he said quietly. "What part does she play in this?"

"She's helping me," I said in a flat voice. "She's trying to discover what's going on."

"How is she—uh—going about it?"

"I'd rather not say."

"Do you meet her secretly?"

"No, it's very important that no one know about our friendship. She writes to me. I—I'd prefer not to talk about it."

Gavin nodded, that preoccupied look back in his eyes. He poured another cup of coffee and sipped it thoughtfully, apparently forgetting all about my presence. I had told him too much. He was a friend, and I trusted him, but from his manner it was obvious that he thought I was mentally disturbed. Was I? Had I indeed put sinister interpretations on a perfectly innocent situation? Had I "imagined" Madame DuBois' spying and the dark form in the ruins? Confused, bewildered, I stood up, wanting to be alone. Gavin put his coffee cup down and stepped over to me. He took my hands in his and held them gently.

"Forgive me, Jane. I'm afraid this hasn't been a very satisfactory talk on your part. You look upset."

"I'm not upset."

My manner was cold and rigid. Gavin squeezed my hands.

"Everything is going to be all right, you know."

"Is it?"

"You're going to get well. I intend to see to that. From now on I want you to think of me as your doctor as well as your friend." Giving my hands another squeeze, he released them and walked with me to the front door. "I can help you, Jane."

"Can you, Doctor Clark?" I said stiffly.

"Only if you'll let me."

"I think not. I don't need your help. Jamintha and I can manage without it. Find another blind boy."

"Jane—" A light frown creased his brow, and there was a worried look in his warm brown eyes. "I—I have to go to London. I thought I'd done all the research necessary, but I find I need to conduct a couple of follow-up interviews before I can finish the chapter I'm working on. I'll be gone for three or four days. I hope you'll have reconsidered by the time I get back. I'm fond of you, Jane, you must know that. Are we still friends?"

"Good-bye, Doctor Clark. I hope you have a pleasant trip."

I was filled with remorse all weekend long. Gavin had been my friend, the first I had ever had besides Jamintha, and I had turned stiff and cold on him simply because he wanted to help me. He was a doctor, evidently a highly skilled one, even if this new field "psychology"—is that what he had called it?—wasn't generally accepted. Perhaps he *could* help me. I had rejected his offer, and in so doing I had rejected his friendship as well. I brooded about that. I learned from Susie that he had, indeed, left for London Friday afternoon in a hired coach from the village. When he returned perhaps it would be possible to repair the breach my own frigid manner had caused. I wondered if I really were mentally disturbed. I thought about Gavin's quiet, gentle voice and his compassionate brown eyes. Perhaps I *should* put myself in his hands ...

It was raining again on Sunday, heavy sheets falling in a steady downpour. I had slept late, and after lunch I found it impossible to sleep. My room was unbearable, the cloying atmosphere depressing. Despite the rain, Charles Danver had gone to the mill, and Susie had informed me that Madame DuBois was staying in her room, suffering from a severe headache. No one would be about. I decided to go down to the drawing room. I could watch the rain through the tall French windows. At least it would be more pleasant than staying here with the walls seeming to press in on me.

I stood at the tall windows, peering through the dripping panes at the rain lashed gardens. I could see the stables, the horses snug and dry in their stalls. I had been standing there silently for over ten minutes when I heard springs creak in one of the chairs and a soft, cushy sound as someone shifted his body. Startled, I whirled around. Brence Danver stared at me from across the room. He was sitting in the shadows, but in the misty light I could see that his face was extremely pale and drawn.

"Hello, Cousin," he said.

"I—I didn't know you were here."

"I didn't wish to intrude on your meditation."

"Nor do I wish to intrude on yours. I'll leave—"

"No need to. Unless you're afraid to stay."

"Why should I be afraid?"

"I'm the big bad wolf, remember?"

"I find your humor singularly unamusing."

"Stiff as ever, prim as a maiden aunt. Look, why don't you relax a little. I'm in a friendly mood at the moment. We could chat. I'm glad to see you up and about."

"I've been up and about for quite some time."

"Well, anyway, I hope you're feeling better."

"I feel fine, thank you." My voice was like ice.

Brence Danver muttered something under his breath, plainly disgusted by my manner. "Forget it," he said. "I'd as soon talk to a box of starch. You have all the personality of a dressmaker's dummy."

"I don't have to stay here and be insulted by you."

"Then get the hell out!"

As I started to leave, I noticed the look in his eyes. It was a sad, defeated look, and he slumped back in the overstuffed chair like a man who has given up all hope. I was strangely moved. Perhaps he actually *wanted* to talk to someone. I walked across the room and took a chair near his, sitting primly with my hands folded in my lap.

"You look ill," I said.

"Do I? Well, I feel like death if that's any satisfaction."

"Do you have a hangover?"

"I haven't touched a drop of liquor in four days."

"Oh?"

"I've decided to give it up! At least I'm gonna try—"

"That's an admirable resolution," I said primly.

He gave me an exasperated look and ran his hand through his dark hair, further dishevelling it. His blue eyes were cloudy with misery, and he seemed different somehow. I realized, then, what it was. All the fire was gone, that passionate vitality quenched. I knew that sudden withdrawal from alcohol frequently had this effect, but it was more than that. Brence Danver had suffered a deep and grievous disappointment, and it had left its mark on him. He wasn't openly abject, but the dejection was there in the slump of his shoulders, in the tight set of his wide mouth, in the way his large hands gripped the arms of the chair.

"I'm sorry," I said quietly.

"For what?"

"For what happened with—that woman."

"You know about that? I suppose you must. Nothing's secret for long in this damned place. I guess the whole village is talkin' about it. Brence Danver's finally had his comeuppance—hooray, bully, bully. Gloat, why don't you?"

"Why should I gloat?"

"Because you must hate my guts. Everyone else does. Don't blame 'em. I'm a pretty despicable guy. Jamintha pointed that out. She told me in no uncertain terms what a shiftless, rotten cad I am. It's true."

"You—you must have loved her."

He didn't answer. He glared down at the carpet, his hands gripping the arms of the chair so tightly that the worn velvet bunched up. The desolation in his intense blue eyes was pitiful to behold. I knew that he really had loved her. He had wanted her physically, wanted her in the worst possible way, but it had gone much deeper than that. I think Brence himself was bewildered by the depths of emotion she had aroused. He looked strangely vulnerable, and I felt an overwhelming impulse to caress his pale cheek and assure him all would be well.

"She threw me over," he said bitterly, "but at least I got somethin' out of it. I got some pretty grim insights."

"Did you?"

"She held a mirror up. I saw myself for the first time."

"That's why you've given up drinking?"

"I just realized I couldn't go on like this. I'm twenty-six years old! I gotta do somethin' with my life. Drinkin' and wenchin' and gettin' into fights—" He shook his head savagely. "My father, I think he's *glad* I'm the way I am. He can feel superior. His wastrel son presents no threat. He makes loud noises of protest, but—hell, why'm I tellin' *you* all this! You couldn't possibly understand."

"Perhaps I do. You—you want to reform so that you can win her back. Isn't that it?"

He laughed a harsh, ugly laugh. "Win her back! I

wouldn't have her! She's a—I couldn't *tell* you what she is, Cousin. You'd have a fit of vapors and topple right out of that chair. She tossed me over all right, and do you know why? Because she's after my father. They're probably together right now."

I lowered my eyes, making no comment.

"I loved her, dammit! I still do. I hate her. I'd like to choke her to death, but I still—" His voice broke. He sat in moody silence for several minutes, staring across the room.

"You'll get over it, Brence," I said in a timid voice.

"Damned right I will! I don't intend to sit around and mope. Tomorrow I'm going to go to the mill. Charles Danver doesn't know it, but I'm going to take over. He's had things his way long enough!"

"Aren't you—afraid of him?"

"I think maybe I was. I'm not any longer! I've made a shambles of my life so far, but that doesn't mean I can't change. He'll raise hell, he'll kick and holler and use all his power to try 'n stop me when he finds out what I intend to do, but that won't matter. The way he runs the place—the way he treats those men—all that's gonna be different, I promise you. If he gets rough, I can get rough too!"

There was a strong resolution in his voice, a determined look in his eyes. Anger had done it. The dejection was gone, vanished as though it had never been, and all the old fire had returned, that intense vitality charging through him once again. I believed he'd succeed. I visualized violent arguments, heated conferences, perhaps even a full scale strike. Once they realized his intentions, the men were sure to rally round Brence. Charles Danver was going to have a fight on his hands, all right, and when it was over, when the final smoke had cleared, I wouldn't be at all surprised to see his son in complete command of the helm. If ever a man breathed fire and brimstone, Brence Danver did now.

"Things're gonna be different," he said grimly.

He might not ever realize it, and he would certainly never acknowledge it, but he owed Jamintha a debt of gratitude. She had succeeded where all else had failed. She had taken a surly, self-centered youth and made a man of him.

Brence sighed, controlling the anger, forcing it deep down where it would remain for a long, long time, fuel for his purpose. He looked up at me, staring intently as though seeing me for the first time. I grew uneasy, discomfited by that intense blue gaze scrutinizing me so closely. He knitted his dark eyebrows together, the corners of his mouth turning up in tight points.

"I feel better," he said sternly, "damned if I don't! Just talking to you helped me get things straight in my mind. You know, Cousin, I think I've underestimated you."

"Indeed?"

"There's something there besides sawdust and starch, after all. This is the first time—hell, this is the first time I've ever felt a woman *understood* me."

An elation welled up inside of me, a joy that seemed to make my whole body light and airy. He was still studying my face with that rude, intense scrutiny, and although my cheeks must have been brushed with a faint pink glow I managed to control that bubbling elation and smother it almost immediately. I was plain Cousin Jane. That's how he would always see me.

"Is it?" My voice was cool and reserved.

"Jamintha didn't. She was toying with me. The others—they're not worth mentioning! I feel you *know* me, Cousin. I feel you're on my side. God knows why, after the way I've treated you."

"You needn't apologize."

"I am, though. I think maybe you and I could be friends, Cousin. I need a friend at this point."

"I—I'd like that."

Brence climbed slowly to his feet, stretching his arms out and throwing his shoulders back, that glorious vitality surging through him, sending off currents. He wore tight gray trousers and a loose white silk shirt that sagged at the waistband where it had been carelessly tucked in. Black boot leather gleamed darkly, and I could feel the warmth of his body, feel the energy charging through it. There was a smell of shaving lotion and the musky odor exclusive to the male. Sitting there in the armchair, so close I could have reached out and touched his leg, I drew back, afraid of the emotions his nearness aroused, afraid he might detect them in my face.

"Right, then," he said amiably, "we'll be good chums."

"Right," I whispered.

Brence smiled. Curling one hand into a fist, he tapped me lightly on the chin, shook his head and sauntered out of the room. I sat there for a long time watching the rain sliver down the window panes. I felt very, very cold inside. That friendly tap of his had demonstrated far better than anything else could have the futility of my true feelings for him.

He wanted a good chum.

I wondered what had transpired this past week, how Jamintha had handled Charles Danver, what she had said to Brence to cause him to harbor such deep resentment and pain. I was soon to find out, for when I woke up the next morning another letter had been slipped under the door.

CHAPTER THIRTEEN

Jane dear,

I hesitate to write this, for I know you'll be shocked by the things I'm about to relate. You live in a safe, secure, tight cocoon, protected by that hard shell, but I'm the butterfly who has burst out. I must fly. I must test my wings. It's delicious, this freedom, this marvelous pure air that allows me to soar . . . There is danger, yes, but I still prefer it to your cocoon, Jane. But enough. I must tell you about this past week and the new developments.

As I told you in my last letter, Charles Danver was to call on me Monday afternoon. I knew it would be a decisive meeting, and I was prepared. It had rained all morning, and the afternoon was bleak and gloomy, a world of gray. I turned on no lamps in the parlor. Calmly, I waited for the sound of a carriage in the street outside, the creak of the gate opening, the heavy tread of footsteps on the porch. That calm may seem unusual under the circumstances, but it was the result of complete confidence in myself . . . and in him.

I wore a violet silk dress with long sleeves and a low, tight bodice, the skirt spreading out below the snug waist like the petals of a flower. My hair was pulled back from my face, fastened behind each temple with a black velvet bow, glossy curls tumbling down in rich waves to the small of my back. I wore a subtle, tantalizing perfume, and there was a touch of coral on my lips. In the blurry silver mirror, my eyes were violet, not blue, and I knew that Charles Danver was going to find me irresistible.

At three o'clock he opened the gate and stepped to the door. I let him knock several times before I opened it. Then, smiling pleasantly, I led him into that parlor so faintly lighted. Moving gracefully, skirt making a silken rustle, I poured brandy from a crystal decanter and handed the glass to him. Neither of us had spoken a word.

He sipped the brandy, staring at me with hard, dark eyes, his face set in stern lines, brows almost meeting over the bridge of his nose, eyelids heavy. I noticed the fleshiness, those too padded cheeks, the little roll of flesh beneath his chin, curiously attractive, adding to an already highly sensual face. He wore a black broadcloth suit, the trousers tucked into the tops of shiny black boots that ended mid-calf; above his jacket the too-elaborate waistcoat of silver satin patterned with embroidered black silk leaves could be seen. He had dressed for the meeting as carefully as I had, the male peacock displaying rich plumage to attract the pea hen. His thick black hair was casually disarrayed. He had a potent, leathery smell, and there was the elusive, unmistakable smell of physical desire. The tenseness was there as well, that slight tightening of the muscles that indicates masculine need.

He set the empty glass down and took a slender black cigar out of his breast pocket. Taking a long match from a jar on the overmantle, I struck it and held the flame for him. He lit the cigar and slowly exhaled tendrils of pale smoke.

"Who are you?" he asked in a ponderous voice.

"I'm the woman your son loves."

"You're not the schoolmaster's sister."

"No."

"I checked that. A few discreet inquiries were all that was necessary. He has a sister, all right, but she's thirty-four years old, pale, skinny and devoted to church work."

"Hardly the type Brence would find interesting," I said. There was a faintly mocking amusement in my voice.

"Who are you?" he repeated harshly.

"Jamintha."

"No last name?"

"Is one really necessary, Mr. Danver?"

"I'll tell you who you are: you're an adventuress. Your mystery shouldn't be too difficult to guess. A man. Perhaps several. You found it necessary to leave the city rather hastily—perhaps to avoid an open scandal, perhaps to avoid involvement in a lawsuit. Or maybe your lover discovered you in some kind of deceit and you simply fled. You came to Danmoor because it's isolated and no one would be likely to look for you in a place like this. Am I right?"

"You could be," I replied.

"You soon discovered that there was only one young man in town worthy of your interest—my son. You learned that he was spoiled, with a deplorable weakness for women, and you set about ensnaring him."

"He made the first move, Mr. Danver."

"I've no doubt you arranged that. You're clever. Women like you are always clever."

"You've had experience with women like me?"

"In my day," he retorted gruffly.

"I can well imagine that," I said.

He looked at me sharply, angry, disturbed. Smiling, I sat down on the sofa, spreading my skirt out. He took a long drag on the cigar and then hurled it into the fireplace. I touched my hair, running my fingers through the glossy chestnut curls. He stared at me. He was an imposing figure, a man who took what he wanted with brutal disregard for others, but I knew I had nothing to fear.

"I wield a great deal of power, young woman. I could have you run out of town. I could have charges brought against you."

"I don't think you'll do that."

"Damn you! If you imagine you can—" He cut himself short, smothering the spurt of rage. He smouldered, fighting the emotions he felt stirring so strongly inside. Charles Danver is a passionate man, but he has learned to master those passions, unlike Brence. Cold, calculating, he knows the value of restraint, and I'll wager he has never once acted on impulse. He's too careful, always in control of himself.

"My son claims he's asked you to marry him. He said you'd refused him. Is that true?"

"Quite true."

"Why? I'd imagine it's one of the few times a man's offered to make an honest woman of you. Your kind—men don't marry your kind. They keep you in perfumed apartments on the Embankment. My son will one day be an extremely wealthy man. Why did you refuse him?"

"Because, Mr. Danver, you son is, as you say, weak and spoiled. He is a boy. I'm not interested in surly little boys."

"No?"

"No," I said quietly.

His chest swelled. The muscles of his face were taut. His powerful hands opened and closed stiffly. I met his stare with a level gaze, and I could feel the tension crackling in the air like a static force. His forehead was slightly damp, and the palms of his hands were moist. A weaker man would have already made some overt gesture, would have crushed me into his arms with clumsy force, but Charles Danver is not weak. That steely control remained. He smiled an icy, sarcastic smile.

"Did you actually believe you could ensnare me too?" His voice was as hard as granite.

"I don't believe anyone could do that, Mr. Danver."

The lie went over well. He felt assured of himself, and of victory. I was, after all, a weak, frail woman in a violet dress, and he was the strong, invincible male, accustomed to command, made to dominate and control. *He* would make the first move. *He* would make the decisions, lay down the rules, and I would obey, meek, submissive, feminine. He knew that I found him attractive. What he did not know was that I could predict his every move. Women know by instinct what most men never learn after a lifetime of experience.

"I'm not a boy," he said huskily.

"I'm well aware of that." My voice was deliberately shaky.

"What kind of game are you playing?"

"Is it—is it so strange that I find you—interesting? I—I saw you driving to the mill in your carriage. Your face was so stern. You held the reins so firmly. You were wearing a check suit that day, and the wind blew your hair across your eyes. I found out who you were. I knew it would be impossible to meet you under normal circumstances—"

"So you used my son. You knew I'd never tolerate—" He nodded, seeing it all now, imagining the young woman standing on the street and seeing him drive past, immediately enamored. His ego swelled and he felt younger than he had felt in years, stronger, a potent young buck despite the thickening waist and the faint double chin.

"You have every reason to despise me," I continued in a wavering voice. "I—I won't see Brence again. You needn't worry."

I stood up, frail, a sad look in my eyes. He didn't miss it. His own eyes were hard, his expression severe. I had appealed to his conceit, and I had won, but he was not to let me off so easily. He had to toy with me a while.

"So you fancy me?" he said in a rough voice.

"I've admitted that. I'm sorry. I should have known—"

"You should have known I'm not to be manipulated like a boy, like my son. I'm not so easily taken in."

"Forgive me, Mr. Danver." My voice was edged with sharpness now. "I made a mistake."

"What do you propose to do now?"

"I suppose I'll leave Danmoor."

"Where will you go?"

"That needn't concern you."

"What if I ordered you to stay?"

"No one orders me to do anything."

"No? That may well be changed."

"You can't—"

"I can do anything I wish. You've made that quite clear."

I turned away from him, pretending anger. Charles Danver seized my arm and whirled me back around to face him. His dark eyes were glowing. He was enjoying this. I tried to pull away, pretending alarm now, for that was what he wanted to see. He smiled a grim smile.

Still holding on to my arm, he curled the fingers of his other hand around my chin, tilting my head back. "Yes—" he said as though to himself, "you're a beautiful minx. I can see why the boy was so smitten. He didn't know how to handle you."

"You're hurting me—" I protested.

"Am I? You'll have to get used to that."

"I'm leaving Danmoor. Tomorrow. I—"

"You'll stay," he commanded.

"W—why?"

"You know the answer to that question."

He released me abruptly, stepping back. Catching his thumbs in his waistcoat pockets, he glanced around the room with disapproval. It wasn't worthy of him, this place. He was envisioning one of those perfumed apartments, for, already, he saw me as merely another possession, to take and use as he willed. His conception of romance—and sex—is purely cliché. A mistress belonged in plush, scented rooms, not a rather shabby, middle-class cottage with doilies and horsehair sofa.

"I'll make arrangements," he said. "I own a small white frame house that will do nicely. It will have to be re-decorated—I'll see to that. This place smells of cabbage."

"And in the meantime?"

"You'll stay here. You'll wait for me to call on you. I may stop by for a short while in the afternoons. I'll expect tea and conversation and a respectful attitude. When the house is ready—" He allowed himself a slight leer of anticipation. Possession would be all the more satisfying for the wait he was imposing on himself.

"We understand each other?" he asked sternly.

"I think so."

"I'll tolerate no disobedience, no coyness."

"Yes, Charles," I said, using his name for the first time. He noticed that. It pleased him. In that preposterous waistcoat, with that smug tight smile on his lips, he looked more than ever like an arrogant peacock.

"What about the Frenchwoman?" I asked.

"She'll present no problem, I assure you."

"You intend to dismiss her?"

"That's none of your business. I like my tea strong. I prefer it to be served with tiny frosted cakes. I like a cigar afterward. Put in a supply of Havanas. Expect me tomorrow at three."

He left without another word, without touching me. I stood in the hall, listening to the carriage driving away, my cheeks flushed with triumph. I felt relief as well. Charles Danver himself had solved my biggest problem. He had too much pride to attempt to make love to me in a place that "smells of cabbage," and my virtue would be quite safe until he had provided a suitable love nest. That would give me plenty of time . . .

He came the next afternoon. I served tea, with tiny frosted cakes, and afterward I lighted his cigar and sat demurely on the armchair across from him. He sat back on the sofa and put his feet up on the coffee table, the picture of a man at ease, but he didn't so much as take off his coat. I suspect that Charles Danver is, deep down, rather stuffy where matters of the heart are concerned. His love-making would be expert, deliberate, perfunctory, with no surprises. Now, smoking his cigar and watching me through the smoke, he looked smug and self-satisfied, like a man who's just pulled off a particularly tricky business deal. When he left an hour later, we had hardly exchanged a dozen words.

On Wednesday afternoon he was a bit more responsive. I got him to talk about the mill. He grew expansive, describing his accomplishments, and I was fascinated, my eyes full of admiration. He relaxed, content, and when he left he rested his hand on my cheek for a moment, peering into my eyes with an indulgent expression. He was beginning to thaw. I was convinced I would have his complete confidence before long, and then I would be able to subtly phrase those questions so important to us.

He hadn't been gone for more than an hour Wednesday afternoon when I heard another carriage pulling up outside. I assumed it was someone visiting one of the neighbors. Although it was still early, the sun was beginning to sink, lingering in deep orange rays on the housefronts. The cottage was filled with a dull orange glow, the furniture darkly outlined. Sitting in the parlor, I thought about Charles Danver. Soon, very soon, he would tell me everything I wanted to know . . .

Suddenly the front door was flung open violently. I leaped to my feet, filled with alarm. The door slammed shut. Angry footsteps sounded in the hall.

Brence stormed into the room.

His rage was magnificent to behold. Eyes snapping with dark blue fire, cheeks pale, nostrils flaring, his mouth a wide slash, he stood with hands rolled into tight fists resting on his thighs. Too angry to speak, he glared at me and tilted forward, his body rocking.

"Brence—" I whispered.

JAMINTHA

"Is it true!" he cried. "Just tell me that!"

"I—you have no right to—"

"He told me! It gave him a malicious pleasure. He smiled mockingly as he said the words. He said—he said you—" His voice was trembling with anger. "Is it true?"

"Yes," I said.

"I don't believe it! I *can't* believe it—"

"It's true, Brence."

He recoiled as though I had struck him. His face was ashen, the skin stretched tightly over his cheekbones. His eyes filled with hurt, and he looked like a little boy who has been unjustly punished. For one brief instant I thought he was going to burst into tears, and then he drew himself up and the muscles of his face tightened and he stared at me with a calm, frosty rage that was far more alarming than any tempestuous outburst could have been.

"I loved you, Jamintha."

"That was your mistake."

"I actually wanted to marry you."

"Do you think any woman who wasn't an utter imbecile would marry you? You're twenty-six years old, but you act like a rapacious sixteen-year-old, totally irresponsible, totally selfish. You've never done an honest day's work in your life. You drink, you carouse, you storm and sulk like a belligerent infant. You flaunt your virility, you call yourself a man, but you're not a man, Brence. No, you're a self-indulgent, deplorably spoiled child."

"Well put," he said.

"You serve absolutely no purpose in life besides

satisfying your own appetites. Oh, you're handsome and appealing, ornamental, I suppose, but you—you have no real worth, Brence."

"Perhaps you're right," he said crisply.

"I could never respect you."

"I find that amusing, coming from you. You've summed up my character nicely, Jamintha. Let me sum up yours. I can do it in one word."

"I know what you must think of me."

"You're a conniving bitch! You used me to get to him. He's going to set you up in a house. He told me. He's already brought in a firm of decorators from London, already! In less than two weeks it'll be ready, and then—damn you, Jamintha! *Damn* you!"

"I don't expect you to understand."

"Is it his wealth, his power?"

"No, I—"

"Then it's pure lust."

"Insult me all you wish, Brence. It won't change anything."

"To think I denied myself, to think I treated you like a decent woman. He told me what you are! You're an imposter, an adventuress. To think I was so easily taken in! I should have— God! What a fool I've been, what a bloody fool, and all the time you were laughing at me!"

"Brence—"

"I should have taken you that first day. I should have treated you like the whore you are! By God, it's not too late—"

He seized my forearms, fingers gripping the flesh like bands of steel, squeezing until I cried out. He jerked my body to him and slammed his mouth over mine with one fierce bend of his neck. All his rage went into that brutal kiss. When I tried to pull away, his fingers tightened even more on my arms, crushing my flesh with savage cruelty. He stumbled, and both of us almost fell, but still his mouth covered mine in that furious, plundering kiss.

Abruptly, he shoved me away from him.

"I'd like to kill you!" he yelled.

I was frightened now, terribly frightened. He looked capable of doing what he said. My breath came in short gasps.

Suddenly, so quickly that I barely saw it coming, he swung his arm in a wide arc, the palm flat and hard, slamming it across my jaw with stunning impact. A chaos of bright, blinding light exploded in front of me. I fell backward, tumbling onto the carpet in a crumpled heap. My eyes smarted with salty tears, lights still whirled in my head, and my jaw burned with agonizing fire where his hand had smashed against it. I moaned, wincing at the excruciating pain.

Minutes passed, long, tormenting minutes, and when I looked up through tear-damp lashes I saw him towering over me. I made no effort to get up. The dizziness had gone now, and my head was clear, but my jaw was still stinging. Brence stared down at me, his mouth curled down at one corner with brutal satisfaction.

"You won't forget me, Jamintha," he said. "You and my father—you deserve each other."

His voice seemed to come from a long way off. I rubbed my jaw, tears still clinging to my lashes. A wave of hair had fallen across my cheek. I brushed it aside.

"I loved you. I wanted to spend the rest of my

life with you. Everything you said about me may be true, probably is, but there was one thing worthwhile—the feeling I had for you."

"Go, Brence," I whispered. "Just go—"

He walked over to the door. Then, his hand resting on the frame, he turned to look at me through the fading orange glow. Catching hold of the arm of the sofa, I pulled myself up, standing on shaky legs. His face was in shadow, all smooth, flat planes. His rage was gone, and he looked exhausted, as though it took a great effort to stand upright. The room was almost dark as the last glow vanished. Brence shrugged his shoulders. It was a pathetic gesture. Curiously enough, I felt closer to him at that moment than I had ever felt before. There was so much I wanted to tell him, so much I couldn't say.

"Good-bye, Jamintha," he said gravely.

And then he was gone. I heard his footsteps in the hallway, heard the front door opening, closing. Pain cut through my body, pain far more agonizing than the physical pain in my jaw and arms. I had a wild impulse to rush after him, to pull at his arm, explain everything, alleviate the hurt I had caused him. I felt as though my heart were being wrenched from my body, and I wished, furiously, that I could be really hard, that I could feel nothing but relief. There was a loud creak as he climbed into the carriage, the noisy clang of horse hooves on the cobbles as he drove away.

That was Wednesday and today is Sunday. Tonight I'll deliver this letter to you.

I've seen Charles Danver three more times. He

JAMINTHA

takes off his coat now. In shirtsleeves and embroidered vest, he drinks his tea and lolls back on the sofa, smoking his cigars, a man at ease with his soon-to-be mistress (or so he thinks!). He devours me with his eyes, anticipating that day he will escort me into that bedroom which, believe it or not, shall be done up in pink satin and ivory. He talks freely now, and I have already begun to ask discreet questions.

He was in an unusually expansive mood on Friday afternoon. He greeted me with a perfunctory kiss, and I helped him off with his jacket. Grumbling a little because I'd forgotten to buy more cakes, he took his tea with bread and butter. The house had already been painted, he informed me, and men were putting up new wallpaper today. Two loads of furniture had arrived, including the ivory bed a man from London had selected.

"Soon, Jamintha," he said huskily.

I blushed modestly. That delighted him. He gave a rich, deep chuckle, patting my shoulder.

"Tell me, Charles," I said casually, "why do you stay on at Danver Hall? It's old and tumbling down and it's bound to be hideously drafty. You could obviously afford to build a more comfortable place. What makes you stay there?"

"I have my reasons," he retorted.

"That horrible ruined wing—why haven't you closed it off?"

He didn't seem to hear me. Setting his cup down, he stared across the room with suddenly distant eyes. I had the impression he'd completely forgotten my presence. He frowned, creasing his brow. "Eleven years—" he said to himself, his voice so low I could barely catch the words. "Eleven years I've been searching. It's there. It has to be. Somewhere in that house, or in the ruins—"

"What, Charles? What have you been searching for?"

The sound of my voice brought him out of his study. Ignoring my question, he sat up straight and pulled out a cigar. I had better sense than to press him, but I was intrigued by that momentary lapse. Eleven years he'd been searching . . . Eleven years since the accident in the west wing. I'm on to something, Jane. I'm making progress. He trusts me now. I flatter his ego. My eyes reflect the image he wants to see. He's growing fond of me. I believe I can make him fall in love with me . . . A man hides nothing from the woman he loves.

Jamintha

CHAPTER FOURTEEN

There could be no mistake this time. I was wide awake and hadn't even made preparations for bed. Not at all sleepy, I had been sitting in the large green chair for some time, thinking about Jamintha's letter which I had received yesterday morning, afraid for her, knowing the risk she was taking in trying to deceive a man like Charles Danver. It was after midnight now. I heard the footsteps clearly. Someone was prowling in the west wing.

Still fully dressed, I turned out the lamp and opened my door cautiously. I was utterly calm, my head clear, my senses sharp. You're not sleepwalking this time, Jane, I told myself as I closed the door behind me and slipped into the velvety darkness of the hall.

Ahead, I could see a faint glimmer of moonlight coming through the opening that led to the west wing. I still heard the footsteps—rather, the echoes of them. They were distant, ringing among the ruins, but the wind carried the noise. I thought, too, that I heard a murmur of voices. Moving quietly, my skirt rustling with a faint, scratchy sound, I approached the pale glow of the opening.

Alert, straining to catch every sound, I drew nearer and nearer, my mouth set in a determined line. The footsteps rang louder, and I distinctly heard voices now, one shrill and vitriolic, one low and rumbling. Both voices were familiar. I peered into the ruined west wing. The figures were moving toward me and I could see the dark shapes in the moonlight. They were leaving the ruins. Quickly, I darted away from the opening, afraid they would see me. I moved into the shelter of a recessed doorway, my heart beating rapidly now. Tensely, I leaned back against the door, staring at the flat silver pool of light not ten yards away. The doorway completely concealed me.

"I won't tolerate it, Charles! You're not going to do this to me. I won't allow it!"

"You have no say in the matter."

"No say! Eleven years of—of *service*. That gives me no say? You're mistaken, Charles. I have plenty of say. If you do this—" In her excitement, her voice was more French, a pronounced nasal accent that I hadn't noticed before marking each word.

"What will you do?" he asked in a bored voice.

"There's plenty I could do!" she cried shrilly.

"Shut up. Someone might hear you."

"Your 'niece?' That pale, timid little mouse? She's bound to be sound asleep, probably drugged. Besides, she's not likely to come investigating the ruins after last time—"

"Lower your voice just the same," he ordered.

JAMINTHA

As they stepped through the opening, I saw that Charles Danver carried a hooded lantern and was wearing a heavy leather coat. Madame DuBois wore a dark wool dress, a voluminous red shawl wrapped around her arms and shoulders. In the moonlight I could see that her face was pinched and strained under the rice powder and rouge. His face was brutal, features granite hard, brows lowered over dark, angry eyes. They were standing so close I could make out every detail.

"*That* was a mistake," she said viciously, "and a waste of time. She can't remember anything, and even if she could—she was seven years old at the time! She couldn't know anything."

"I'm not so sure," he said soberly. "She may remember something very important."

"What could she possibly remember?" she snapped shrewishly.

"Jeanne may have told her something."

"A seven-year-old child?"

"She may even have given it to her to hide."

"Preposterous!"

Huddled there in the shadows, I tuned their voices out. I could hear the silken rustle of skirts, and I could hear her laughter, such gay, irrepressible laughter, and it seemed I could smell her perfume . . . Jeanne, pronounced "John," Jeanne, yes, I remembered now. Long blonde hair, silvery blonde, and flirtatious blue eyes, a soft pink mouth that could be coy or severe. My adopted father adored her, her devoted slave, and the other men were irresistibly drawn to her. There were many men, house guests, friends, and she loved to joke with them, loved to have them gathered around her, broad shoulders and backs concealing her from the little girl who tried to be as flirtatious, as gay as she . . . These impressions flashed into my mind like lightning and vanished as quickly. For one split second I had remembered her vividly.

Charles Danver's heavy voice intruded.

"I'll find it. It's got to be here."

"You're obsessed!" she exclaimed. "All these years—prowling in the ruins at night, searching. Going over every room in the house. Eleven years devoted to—"

"The greatest treasure hunt in history." He cut her short. "Are you able to comprehend what it would mean if we found it—*when* we find it? A king's ransom, more than that! Wealth that staggers the imagination."

"I don't care about that!" she exclaimed. "Charles, this woman—"

"I find her amusing."

"Amusing!"

"Intriguing might be a better word. She intrigues me."

"She's common, a common adventuress. It's your money she's interested in—"

"I think she loves me," he said bluntly. "I think I might easily fall in love with her."

He spoke the words with cruel satisfaction. Helene DuBois drew back, each word a knife wound. She looked at him with frantic eyes. Returning her look with one of indifference, Charles Danver sighed, clearly bored with this skinny, painted woman he had used so long. He was completely unmoved by the anguish in her eyes and in her voice.

"She makes me feel important. She makes me feel like a man. It's been a long time since I've felt this way. Since Jeanne, in fact."

"How dare you say these things to me. How dare you! You delight in tormenting me. You saw the way she treated Brence. She'll treat you the same way. I won't permit it. I—"

"It's none of your concern."

"Isn't it? *Isn't* it? I've lived for you. Your every wish—at your beck and call. I've kept this horrible ruin from falling down about our heads. I've managed the household accounts. I've been there, waiting, whenever you felt—" Her voice grew louder and shriller, a long nasal shriek now. "I'll not be pushed aside by some common little strumpet who happened to catch your eye! You're not going to—"

He slapped her once, a healthy, vigorous blow, not really vicious, and the shriek died in her throat. In the bulky leather coat he looked larger than ever, undeniably menacing, but Helene DuBois gave no indication of being intimidated. She wrapped the flowing red shawl more tightly around her arms, and there was a curious dignity about her as she looked at him with eyes that seemed suddenly dead and lifeless.

"I won't permit it, Charles," she said. Her voice was quiet now, so low I had to strain in order to make out the words. "I know too much about you. I was there, remember. I saw. Don't think I would hesitate to tell if I had to—"

"That, my dear, would be a drastic mistake."

Turning away from her, he walked slowly, ponderously down the hall, the lantern swinging in his hand. Helene DuBois stood in the moonlight, an anguished expression on her face. Clutching the shawl about her, she listened to his footsteps growing fainter and fainter in the distance. I was startled to see tears streaming down her thin cheeks. I had despised this woman, yet now I felt a great sympathy for her. I understood her for the first time. Giving a low, animal-like sob, she hurried off after the man who was the sun of her existence.

I returned to my room, shaken by what I had seen and heard.

Dawn was breaking when I awoke the next morning. After ringing for Susie, I began to dress. I was braiding my hair when she entered, surprised to see me up so early.

"I think I'll take my breakfast in the drawing room, Susie," I said. "Could you bring my tray there?"

"Certainly, Miss Jane. I must say, you're looking chipper this morning, and up so *early,* too. Why, Cook 'n I haven't even taken breakfast to the others yet. I'm *pleased,* Miss Jane."

In the drawing room, I ate the toast and crisp bacon and drank two cups of steaming hot coffee. The sun was fully up now, pale yellow light illuminating a pearly sky. I could hear distant, muffled sounds of someone moving around in the east wing, and from the kitchen there came the noisy clatter of crockery.

Pushing the tray aside, I thought about last night.

I had been right. All this time he had been searching for something, something extremely valuable. He had prowled the ruined west wing during the nights—that explained the mysterious lights, the reason superstitious villagers thought the place was haunted—and he and Helene DuBois had gone over every room in the house. He had devoted eleven years to this search, and now, as a last resort, he had brought me here, hoping I would remember something that would lead him to—what? It was farfetched, yes, but it was true. Undeniably. Exactly as I'd outlined it to Gavin that day in his study last week. I felt like rushing out to tell him, but Gavin hadn't returned from London yet.

I must have been sitting there over an hour when I heard the footsteps in the main hall. The connecting doors were open, and although I couldn't see them I could hear their voices clearly. Charles Danver was brusque and cold. Brence's voice was calm and faintly mocking.

"I'll not have you calling Granger aside for conferences, Son. I'll not have you countermanding my orders. I'm pleased that you've finally begun to show an interest in the mill—high time, too—but you're going at it the wrong way."

"Am I, Father?"

"You show far too much concern for the men. They know exactly what to expect, exactly what to do. You can't coddle 'em, Son. You can't treat 'em like pals."

"I just want to treat them like human beings."

"As for remodeling the sheds, it's completely out of the question. Improper ventilation indeed! These men have worked for years without windows, and they'll continue to do so. I want 'em to work, not to stare out at the scenery. They get enough fresh air. The way you talk, a person'd think they were passing out from suffocation."

"Several of them have," Brence said icily.

"And your talk about splitting them into three shifts, nonsense!"

"With three shifts, you'd get more work accomplished. The men wouldn't keep such long hours. When they came in, they'd be fresher—"

"I'd advise you to leave these matters to me, Brence. You've been two days at the mill—today'll be your third day—and already you want to revolutionize the whole place. I know these men. I know how to keep 'em in line."

"I wonder," Brence retorted.

"Brence, this attitude of yours—I don't like it. You keep it up and there'll be trouble. I mean that."

The front door opened, closed, and a few minutes later there was the sound of a carriage pulling around the side of the house. Brence had been as good as his word. He had already started his campaign to change conditions at the mill, and already his father was protesting. I wondered if Brence truly was a man on the road to reform or if this was merely a phase, a reaction to his experience with Jamintha. Would he really carry out his plans, or would he take a first drink, then a second, and soon revert to his old ways? It would be interesting to watch . . .

I wasn't aware that Helene DuBois had come into the room until I heard her clearing her throat, a noise intended to gain my attention. She stood a few feet away, looking haggard in a purple taffeta dress that seemed to drain the color from her face. Her eyelids were coated with mauve shadow, her lips painted scarlet, but these artificial colors only emphasized the stark bone white of cheeks and forehead. She seemed nervous, the icy hauteur completely missing this morning.

"I went to your room. Susie was making the bed. She said you'd come down here to have your breakfast."

"You wished to see me?" I inquired.

She hesitated, glancing over her shoulder to make sure that no one was eavesdropping, and then she came closer, a determined expression on her thin face. I could tell that she had been crying, and once again I was surprised that this bizarre woman with her outlandish clothes could experience genuine emotions. I had considered her a caricature, not a person. She was all too human now as she sat down in a chair facing mine.

"There are things I must tell you—" she said nervously—"things you should know. I—I've kept them to myself far too long. Now he—you have a right to know."

"What is it, Madame DuBois?"

She glanced across the room at the opened doorway, then turned her attention back to me. I could sense her anxiety, and I could see that she was trying to compose herself.

"You wish to tell me something?" I prompted quietly.

"You should know. You should know everything. I'll start at the beginning. When you asked me about your mother, I lied. I said I didn't know her—but I did."

"You knew her well?"

"She was my best friend. I was a widow, her traveling companion. When she married George Danver and came to Danver Hall, I accompanied her. I had nowhere else to go, you see, no one to turn to. I was destitute, but Jeanne was fond of me, and she was loyal. She made a place for me here. I was officially the 'housekeeper,' but actually I remained the close friend, the confidante. She needed someone to talk to, someone to discuss her love affairs with—"

"Love affairs? But she was married—"

A thin smile played on her lips. "Jeanne was one of the most beautiful women of her day. She was born to be a great courtesan. At ten she was a coy flirt, at fifteen she possessed worldly wisdom far beyond her years, at twenty she had more experience than most women ever acquire. She couldn't live without men, without their admiration and desire. She wasn't immoral, she simply couldn't live by normal standards. The de Soissons were all like that—"

"De Soisson," I said to myself. That explained the book upstairs in my room, the history of the de Soisson family that I hadn't finished reading yet.

"Jeanne was lighthearted, amusing, frivolous, generous, kind, and the charm—no woman should have such charm. She moved in a special kind of radiance, dazzling everyone without the least effort. She was also foolish, unwise, impetuous. She fell in love too easily, and she suffered for it, and she never learned. She loved your father. He was dashing in his uniform, an Englishman, one of Her Majesty's Dragoons. Captain Robert Standish—tall and blond and utterly ruthless with women. She wanted to marry him. He laughed at her, and, when he discovered she was pregnant, he deserted her. He shipped to India and died of the fever before you were ever born."

I sat very quietly, listening to this woman. I was calm. I felt no emotion as I absorbed her words. Later, I could think about these things and react to them, I could feel sadness and grief, but now I forced myself to listen with cool objectivity.

"She met George Danver almost immediately after Robert left. He was a man of integrity, honest, upright, decent, and dull, full of good intentions, but so dull. Jeanne married him. She admired him for what he was. She respected him. I think she even loved him in her fashion."

"In her fashion," I repeated in a flat voice.

"There were others, of course. There were balls and parties. Danver Hall was filled with festive gaiety, chandeliers burning, laughter ringing in the hallways, women in flowered gowns—and men, a great many men. They came from neighboring counties, from London, a few even came from France. There were constant house guests, constant games, music—" She broke off, an introspective look in her eyes as she remembered those days.

"George worshiped her. He knew of her affairs. He tolerated them because he couldn't stand the thought of losing her. She would have left him from the very beginning had it not been for you. She loved you with all her heart. She didn't treat you like a child. She treated you like a boon companion, a little friend. She dressed you in silks, showed you off at all the parties. You imitated her. You were a miniature Jeanne, as flirtatious, as coy. You used to flirt with the stable boys—"

"I was like her?"

"In many ways. You were an intelligent child—Jeanne was never intelligent—and sometimes you would slip away and roam over the moors, serious and moody, but those moods never lasted for long. You were very close to George Danver. He treated you like a princess, lavishing you with attention and affection, never acknowledging the fact that you weren't his very own. Jeanne appreciated that. He gave you his name, gave you a home. She stayed with him because of you."

Her face hardened. She leaned forward in the

chair, her body tense. "And then Charles came. He was the younger brother. He resented the fact that George had inherited Danver Hall and the textile mill. He'd left Danmoor years before, squandering his own inheritance in unsuccessful business ventures. He was a widower, with a fifteen-year-old son. He had no money, no prospects, but he knew his brother wouldn't turn him away."

She paused for a moment, remembering. "He was as handsome as a god in those days, full of vitality, the most exciting man I had ever seen. He paid no attention to me, of course. He had eyes only for Jeanne, and she responded to him immediately. He hadn't been here two days before—" She broke off, her eyes reflecting the emotions she had felt eleven years ago. "I resented her. For the first time, I resented her. She had so much, and I had nothing. She was in love again, madly in love, like someone who had had too many glasses of champagne. Then she discovered that he intended to supplant his brother, take over the mill. Jeanne was appalled. Loyalty to George sobered her, ended that mad intoxication. She and Charles had a furious argument. That night, at the dinner table, she told George, and for once he showed backbone. He ordered Charles to leave. Charles assured him that Jeanne was merely being hysterical. He wasn't interested in the mill, he said—and he wasn't, not any more—for that night Jeanne was wearing the—"

"Yes?" Charles Danver inquired casually.

Helene DuBois almost fainted. Her eyes filled with panic. He stood in the doorway, leaning his shoulders against the frame, an indolent, faintly amused expression on his face. I had no idea how long he might have been standing there, how much he might have heard.

"Go on, my dear," he said lazily. "I find your story quite fascinating."

"Charles—" she said hoarsely.

We both stood up as he sauntered into the room. Madame DuBois trembled visibly. Her left hand clutched her skirt, fingers noisily crushing purple taffeta. "Tonight," she whispered frantically. "After dinner, in your room—" I barely heard the words that escaped her lips. Arching one dark brow, smiling amiably, Charles Danver stepped over to his desk and picked up a thin brown leather portfolio.

"I forgot this," he said pleasantly. "I thought I'd better come back for it. Don't let me interrupt anything. Go on with your story, Helene. I'm sure Jane must be intrigued."

She stared at him for one panic-stricken moment, and then she hurried out of the room. Charles Danver shook his head in mock bewilderment.

"Peculiar woman," he remarked. "After all these years I've never been able to figure her out. She seemed unusually tense. I wonder why? Sorry to have broken in like this, Jane, but I really do need this portfolio."

He checked to see that the papers were inside, refastened it, gave me a pleasant nod and sauntered back out of the room.

I wandered over the moors that morning, thinking of all Madame DuBois had told me, anxious to hear the rest of her story. I was certain "that night" was the night of the accident, the night Jeanne de Soisson Danver and her husband had died. Touching the mottled bark of a dwarfed tree, leafless limbs swaying in the wind above me, I stared across the gold and brown land, stark in the brilliant morning sunlight. My father was a Dragoon, blond, English, dashing, heartless. My mother was amoral, a lovely, vibrant creature radiating charm and allure. She had loved me. I had imitated her . . . If only I could remember.

Something bothered me. Something Helene DuBois had said had struck a responsive cord. What was it? For one brief second all the pieces of the puzzle had come together, and everything had been clear. For that one split second I had almost seen the complete picture, the answer, and then, before I could examine it the picture had shattered, the pieces falling apart in a scattered jumble. Something she had mentioned . . . the answer had been there, tantalizingly close, just out of reach. Tonight . . . I would have all the answers tonight.

There was a hollow feeling in the pit of my stomach. My nerves seemed to be strung tight. Curious, this feeling. I had no headache. I wasn't tired. Then what was it? It was several minutes before I realized that it was fear. I was afraid.

I was afraid of what I knew I would hear tonight.

I slept soundly that afternoon. I didn't awaken until after seven. My room was dark with a misty gray darkness, not yet night. Lighting all the lamps, I rang for Susie, and she soon appeared with my dinner tray. Her amiable chatter got on my nerves a bit. Mister Charles had already returned and would be having dinner shortly, but Mister Brence was still at the mill. Will wonders never cease? He was taking *such* an interest in the men's welfare. Madame DuBois was in her room, had been all day, hadn't even rung for lunch. Odd, but then *everyone* knew why she was acting so moody.

"That woman," she said knowingly.

"You talk too much, Susie," I said irritably.

"He goes to her cottage almost every afternoon," she continued, unable to resist such delicious gossip. "What's *more,* he's having that small white house on the edge of town redecorated. A whole fleet of men from London have been working night and *day.*"

"That doesn't concern you, Susie."

"I know, but it's so *juicy!* The whole village is talking about it. She's *shame*less, that woman. First the son, now the father—"

Frowning, I finished the meal. Susie stacked the dishes on the tray, a thoughtful look in her dark brown eyes. "Poor Madame," she said. "I've never liked her, no one has, but I can't help but feel sorry for her. A lot of people do. At least she never *flaunted* their affair."

She left. It wasn't yet eight. It might be an hour before Helene DuBois came to my room, perhaps two. I was tense, every minute stretching out tediously, each second seeming sixty. I wandered about the room restlessly, listening for any telling noise in the hallway outside. Of course that wasn't her, that creaking of floorboards. It was only eight-ten. She would wait until Charles Danver had finished his meal, gone to his room for the night. There. Someone was approaching. No, no, it was merely the normal noises of an old house settling. Eight-fifteen now. Only five minutes had passed? It seemed like an hour.

Outside the sky was black. The wind sounded particularly mournful this evening, almost human, a chorus of lost souls in torment. Nervous fancies. I must get hold of myself. I peered out the window. I straightened up the objects on the dressing table, aligning ivory brush and comb and hand mirror. The lamps cast flickering gold shadows on the walls. I watched the shadows leap and dance. I glanced at the clock. Eight-twenty now. This was absurd. I . . . why should I feel this—this *premonition?* I sat down in the large chair, trying not to tremble.

The beautifully bound history of the de Soissons was on the table beside me, a ribbon marking the place where I had stopped reading. I picked it up, hoping it would help pass the time away. The words took on a new glamor now, a new significance, for now I knew these people were my ancestors. I turned the pages, reading about Jacques de Soisson, the handsome rogue who had cut such a spectacular figure in the court of Louis XVI. Rumor had it that he was the lover of Countess De La Motte-Valois, that intriguing siren who had been so deeply involved in the affair of the Queen's necklace. Absorbed now, I forgot all about the clock.

I knew the story of the Queen's necklace, of course. The subject of a fantastic intrigue and immense political scandal, the necklace, still unpaid for, disappeared and was never located, one of the great mysteries of history and a contributing factor to the Revolution four years later. Especially set for Marie Antoinette, purchased under a cloak of secrecy from the court jeweler, the diamonds had been delivered to Cardinal Prince de Rohan, who gave them to Countess De La Motte-Valois, believed to be the mistress of the dazzling Jacques. A messenger arrived, claiming to have been sent by the Queen. The Countess handed the glittering necklace to him, and it was never seen again. Shortly after the scandal broke, Jacques fled to England. Was he the "messenger," in appropriate disguise? Although there was no proof of it, the author believed it was highly possible that Jacques de Soisson had indeed made off with the fabled jewels.

Caught up in the story of that incredible theft, I had read almost a hundred pages without being aware of it. I was alarmed to see that it was twelve minutes past ten. How could I possibly have become so absorbed? And where was Madame DuBois? I set the book aside. My earlier apprehension came flooding back. She should have been here long before now. What could have happened to her?

Could I possibly have misunderstood those faintly whispered words? Had she said "your room" or "my room?" Perhaps she was in her room now, waiting for me, anxious, worried that I hadn't shown up. I knew I couldn't sit here any longer. I had to see her. I had to hear the rest of that story that had been cut off so abruptly as Charles Danver made his presence known.

Picking up one of the lamps, holding it by the curved brass handle, I left my room. The house was silent and I could smell dampness and mildew and rotting velvet. As I moved through layers of darkness, I had the silly notion that someone was watching me, that someone was going to leap out of one of the darkened doorways. It was nerves, of course, just nerves, but my heart was pounding and I felt extremely vulnerable ... and afraid.

The fear mounted, and I couldn't shake it. Standing at the head of the staircase leading down into the main hall, my nerve completely left me. I stared down into the stairwell. Could I possibly move through that nest of shadows? The lamp didn't help at all. It merely made me more vulnerable, exposing me. I squared my shoulders. I had to see Madame DuBois. I had to hear the rest of her story.

I moved slowly down the staircase, and my flesh seemed to creep as I crossed the main hall and started toward the east wing. The air was cold on the main floor, and the wind blew furiously against the windows, causing them to rattle in their frames. I had never been to Madame DuBois' room, but I knew where it was located. I walked down a long corridor. I could feel currents of icy air and realized that someone must have left one of the windows open. Moving through an archway, treading on thick carpet that gave under my feet, I passed into the east wing.

A gust of wind swept down the hallway. The lamp spluttered violently. The flame leaped and danced for half a second. Then it went out. Darkness enveloped me. I thought I was going to faint. I actually closed my eyes and swayed for a moment as my knees turned watery. I leaned against the wall and the dizziness cleared and the black veils lifted from my mind and I opened my eyes, amazed that my heart could beat so loudly and so rapidly without bursting.

My eyes gradually became accustomed to the darkness. I could see shadowy doorways but no slab of light showed under any of the doors. Charles Danver and Brence were surely asleep, but shouldn't there be a light under her door? Would she be waiting for me in a darkened room? Which room was it? The second from the right. Peering through the gloom I could see it, the polished doorknob gleaming dully.

Calmer now, my heart beating normally, I moved quickly over to the door and knocked lightly. I could hear someone stirring inside, the crisp rustle of material. Relieved, I waited, eager to be out of the dark hallway, eager to hear the rest of her story. The rustling noise continued, but no fan of light appeared beneath the door, no footsteps sounded. I knocked again, louder this time. Perhaps she hadn't heard the first knock.

One minute passed, then two. She did not open the door, and I knew she must have heard my knock. My flesh was suddenly cold and clammy. I felt a tingling sensation along my spine. I knew, I *knew*, even before I turned that doorknob and stepped into the room.

It was flooded with bright silver-blue moonlight. One of the windows was wide open, the draperies flapping in the wind, billowing out, falling back, rustling. I called her name softly, but I knew she wouldn't answer my call. I *knew*. I could feel the malevolence, an atmosphere so thick and real it was almost overwhelming. It seemed to seep from the woodwork and hang in the air like an invisible pall. The room itself breathed evil, retained the impressions of what had happened here. What I had felt earlier, those nervous fancies, were as nothing compared to the sheer, stark horror that gripped me as I stood in the middle of that room.

Hands trembling, I re-lighted the lamp. The room was neat and tidy. The bed was made up, satin counterpane gleaming smooth. There was a slapping, sucking noise as the long draperies flapped in the wind. The air was as cold as icy water, but I hardly noticed it. I was looking at the small mahogany table with the marble top. A bottle of ink rested on the table, an old-fashioned quill pen in an onyx holder, a piece of pale blue paper with three words scribbled over it:

Charles, Forgive me.

The door of the storage closet wasn't securely closed. It hung open perhaps two inches. I touched the doorknob with frozen fingers. The door swung open, creaking loudly. I raised the lamp. She was wearing the same purple dress she had worn this morning. A stool had been turned over on the floor directly beneath her feet. Looking up, I saw the strong black cord fastened to a rafter. I saw her head hanging limply to one side, her face almost as purple as the dress, her eyes wide open, her tongue hanging out. The body dangled in space, swinging back and forth. As my screams filled the air, I don't think I even realized they came from my own throat.

CHAPTER FIFTEEN

Far, far away I could hear voices. They were strangely distorted, diffused. Heavy, solemn, muffled through gauze, Charles Danver spoke. "Yes, she discovered the body, Constable. Great shock. Went to pieces. I carried her back here to her room and sent for Doctor Green immediately."

"Dreadful thing, dreadful," the constable replied.

"Will you need a statement from my niece?"

"Not necessary. It was suicide, no question about it. That note—"

"I feel terrible about this."

"Understandable. The woman was obviously deranged."

"She'd been acting—peculiar for quite some time, but I never expected anything like—"

Something terrible had happened. What? It didn't matter. It surely wasn't important. The clouds drifted, and I sank deep into their billowing substance. Something ugly was trying to tear the clouds from under me and send me hurtling into the abyss. I tensed. I moaned. A hand stroked my forehead. I could see Susie's face suspended above me, and then it was gone and I was floating again.

"How is she?" It was Brence.

"She's still under." Her voice was sharp. "I may as well tell you, Master Brence—Johnny wants me to leave this place. He doesn't like me being here, not one bit. Far too many things've been happening. Cook's already gone, bag and baggage. Left first thing this morning—"

"You're going, too?"

"And leave Miss Jane in this condition? I should say not! As soon as she gets well, maybe, but not until. I told Johnny so. He says—well, I needn't tell you what he says."

"I want you to watch over her, Susie. I've got to go to the mill today. It's absolutely necessary. I probably won't be back until late."

"And Mister Charles?"

"He's in the village, making—arrangements. Will she be all right? What did Green say?"

"He gave her a healthy dose of laudanum. She slept all night. She'll probably sleep the rest of the morning. There's no need for you to hang about here, Master Brence."

"You're a good girl, Susie. I intend to see that you're rewarded for this."

The voices faded. The clouds began to evaporate. I groaned. I opened my eyes. I was in my bed. The room was filled with bright sunshine, but everything was distorted, seen through the mist. The tall white wardrobe seemed to expand, growing fat and rubbery, and the large green chair melted. The carpet undulated like waves. My cheeks were hot. My hair was damp with perspiration. Curiously objective, I watched the walls billow like the walls of a tent, and somewhere deep inside of me a calm voice informed me that it was all right, it was the laudanum wearing off. *Laudanum is a polite name for opium, Jane. Remember Coleridge and "Kubla Khan," De Quincey and his bizarre visions.*

"You're awake," Susie said.

"Yes."

"How do you feel?"

"I'm still a bit foggy."

"I've brought some soup. I made it myself. Cook left. She won't be back."

"Leave it, Susie."

"Now I want you to eat it, Miss Jane. You need it. I'm going to sit right here until you've eaten every bite."

I ate the soup. I had a curious sensation that I was underwater, that Susie and I were on the bottom of a clear, crystal pool, and I thought it strange that I could be eating the soup, that we could both be here down below surrounded by clear rippling waves and not be wet. I set the bowl aside and frowned. I spoke, but my voice sounded distant.

"She killed herself—"

"Try not to think of it, Miss Jane."

"But she didn't, you see. Not really."

"That drug hasn't worn off yet. You'd better try to sleep."

"That's what he wanted people to believe. *He* did it—"

"Now, Miss Jane—"

"I *knew* it. I knew it before I opened that door—"

Gentle hands pushed me back onto the mattress. A soft palm brushed a damp lock from my forehead.

I closed my eyes, hoping to find the soft pink comfort, the light golden glow, but there was only blackness. I could feel the heat withdrawing from my body. I grew cold. Susie was gone now, and I was getting out of bed, hunting for the key, finding it beneath a stack of linen handkerchiefs . . . I slept heavily, deeply, and when I opened my eyes it was late afternoon. I was very, very tired. I closed my eyes again, my lids heavy, shutting out the light.

"Jane?"

Her voice was soft, dream-like.

"You've come," I whispered.

"There was no time to write another letter."

"Jamintha, he—"

"I know. He came to see me this afternoon. He was upset. I gave him brandy. He drank far too much. He said he was in love with me. He said he had to kill her. She was going to tell you about that night—"

"He told you?"

"The brandy hit him hard. He finally passed out. I left him sprawled out there on the sofa."

"What are we going to do?"

"Jane—the necklace. He told me about—"

"I don't remember. I *can't* remember—"

"You must."

"Please don't go away. Don't leave me."

"You must remember, Jane."

"Jamintha—"

Light streamed through the window. The furniture cast long black shadows. I sat up in bed, completely awake now. My head was perfectly clear, and there was a hard core of calm inside. It was an icy calm, resolute. I got out of bed and dressed. I sat at the mirror and began to braid my hair. The eyes that stared back at me in the mirror were perfectly level. My face was composed. It had happened during my sleep.

I remembered everything.

I was in her sitting room, waiting for her to come back. I was upset, because I had heard her arguing with Uncle Charles. Neither of them had been aware that I was sitting in the vast armchair in the drawing room when they came in, shouting at each other. I waited now, huddled in the corner of the lemon velvet sofa. I wanted her to read a story to me. I wanted her to tell me everything would be all right. I could hear her footsteps in the hall. She stopped. There were other, heavier footsteps.

"He told you to leave, Charles. He wants you gone by morning. Don't you think you'd better start packing?"

"I'll leave, Jeanne, but I intend to take something with me."

"What?"

"The necklace. George can have the house. He can have the mill. But I want the necklace."

"What are you talking about? What necklace—"

"The one you were wearing at dinner tonight. I know all about it."

"How could you—"

"I couldn't sleep the other night. I picked up a book from George's study. *The de Soissons*. Very interesting, particularly the chapter about Jacques and his flight to England. Tonight, when I saw that necklace around your lovely throat—"

"You think I'd let you have it? You're insane! It belongs to me. It's been in my family for—"

"You're going to give it to me, Jeanne."
"Why should I? You're stark raving mad—"
"I intend to have it."
"Get out of my way, Charles. Get out of this house."

She came hurriedly into the room. She slammed the door behind her and locked it. Her cheeks were flushed a blazing pink, and she looked afraid. I started crying. She held me tightly in her arms and rocked me, and I must have fallen asleep, for the next thing I knew I was in my own bedroom with the gaily striped wallpaper. The dolls were sitting helter-skelter on top of the bureau. I sat up, rubbing my knuckles over sleepy eyes. A lamp was burning. My mother had come into the room. I smiled at her, and then I saw that her face was drawn and pale. She was crying. She had a handful of stars, glittering stars, sparkling bright with all the colors of the rainbow.

"They're fighting—Charles will kill him! He has a gun! Jane, you must take this necklace. You must hide it. Quickly, quickly!"

She thrust the stars into my hands. She was frantic. She rushed out of the room. I tumbled out of bed and hurried across the floor, my long flannel nightgown dragging. She wasn't in the hall. She had vanished. I heard loud, angry voices coming from a distant room. I started to sob. I clutched the heavy glittering beads in my small hand. I couldn't understand what was happening. Mother . . . she wanted me to hide them. Uncle Charles wanted to steal them. I must hide them well so that he'd never be able to find them . . .

Calmly, so calm, I wound the braids into a tight

coronet and fastened them with pins. Eleven years of amnesia had fallen away, a dark blank spot in my mind had been filled in, and I understood what had done it. When I opened that closet door, when I stared at the hideous sight in front of my eyes, the shock had jolted me, a wall had come tumbling down, and I remembered another hideous sight. The drug had held it in abeyance for a while, opium shrouding my mind with false, feverish serenity. The drug had worn off, but the memory remained.

Cool, objective, I knew that I should be hysterical. I should be weak, but I was strong, stronger than I had ever been before. I should be terrified, but there was no fear. There was no room for anything inside but this singleness of purpose. I would get the necklace. It would serve as proof. I would see to it that Charles Danver was punished, not just for one murder but for three.

Leaving my room, I moved unhurriedly down the back hall. The light was deepening as the sun went down, but there was no need for a lamp. I would have plenty of time to fetch it and return to my room before dark. The huge old wardrobe stood in the hall, almost blocking the passage. I squeezed past it, noting that the enormous doors were still wedged tight. Farther down the hall, Susie's door stood open, but the tiny room was empty. She was probably in the kitchen, I thought, moving on toward the backstairs.

There was a loud creak far behind me, as though someone had placed too much weight on one of the old floorboards. Startled, I turned around and swept the hall with my eyes. Something flickered. It seemed that my heart actually stopped beating for a second as I stared at that dense thickness of shadows. Was someone crouching there? Had someone been following me? Imagination, I decided, scolding myself. I had imagined it all. Still, the incident unnerved me and I felt a curious apprehension.

I found the kitchen empty, too. The deep red tiles gleamed darkly in the fading sunlight. The fireplace was a cavernous black hole. The copper pans shone dully. There was a heavy silence. "Susie," I called, but there was no answer. Where could she have gone? Why would she have left without coming to my room and telling me? It wasn't like her. Standing in the middle of the room, I frowned, worried by her absence. There was probably some perfectly logical explanation, yet I was disturbed nevertheless. I had been so calm in my room, so resolute, and now . . . I heard another creak, from the backstairs this time. Someone hovered there, listening. "Susie," I called again. The word echoed in the silence. No one was there. My nerves were on edge, causing me to imagine things.

I moved through the swinging wooden door. It made a soft swoosh as it swung back into place. I walked down the long, narrow corridor that led into the main hall. The staircase was already becoming the nest of darkness it had been the previous night when I had hesitated to come down it. The house was still, too still. Nothing stirred. Nothing moved. It might have been abandoned for years. The silence was heavy, pressing in on me, broken only by the sound of my breathing.

And then, far behind me, there was a soft swoosh.

I tensed, waiting. Standing beneath the great chandelier, I waited for what seemed an eternity, but there was no repetition of the noise, and there was no sound of stealthy footsteps. Satisfied that no one crouched there in the darkness, I proceeded across the hall and turned down the long corridor that ran the length of the west side of the main house.

It had been a long time since I had come this way, it seemed. I had been at Danver Hall for less than two weeks. I had been upset by my first encounter with Brence, unaware that I was shortly to have another, even more dramatic encounter. It seemed so long ago, a lifetime ago. So much had happened since then. The man who had so arrogantly demolished me that morning now wanted me to be his chum. In my heart, I knew that I preferred his disdain to patronizing friendship.

Turning the corner, I saw the huge mahogany doors. They were locked. I pushed and shoved in vain, frustrated by this obstacle. I wasn't going back to my room empty-handed. I would get into the library even if I had to break these doors down. While this melodramatic determination was highly commendable, common sense told me that such a course would be virtually impossible. The doors were solid, hardened by age. A robust man in his prime could have battered against them with little result beyond fatigue. There was a simpler way to gain entry, and it took me but a moment to think of it. Leaning my head down, I pulled out one of the long hair pins that secured my braids in place.

The lock was old and rusty, and the task wasn't easy. The pin jammed, twisted and broke, making a loud grating noise. I pulled out another and inserted it into the hole, probing less vigorously, with a more delicate touch. After five minutes of scratching and scraping, there was a satisfying click and the heavy doors swung inward with a painful creaking.

The dust-covered shapes of furniture were like so many ghosts crouching in the dim semi-light, and the fetid odor of dust and rotting leather and yellowing paper seemed to make a physical assault. Moving to the center of the room, I stared up at the towering walls of decaying books. As I stood in the ruined room memories came flooding back. I had loved this room—the woodwork had shined with polish back then, the books new and inviting, the large bronze and red globe on its golden oak stand an intriguing toy. The galleries had been sturdy, reinforced with tall pillars since destroyed, and I had been fascinated by the hidden staircase winding up in the hollow tower. Many a rainy afternoon I had spent here, stretched out on the carpet in front of a roaring fire, turning through the picture books that were so plentiful. It had been my favorite room, and I had come here that night . . .

A little girl in a long flannel nightgown that trailed behind her, her cheeks streaked with tears, her hand clasping the heavy strand of diamonds that blazed like silver fire, like stars. She had come running into this room, her bare feet slapping against the carpet. She had gone over to that corner, pressed the near-invisible knob, started up that cold iron staircase curling up into the darkness . . . I could feel her panic now. I could feel her heart pounding, and I could hear her sobs as she climbed higher and higher. No, it was my own heart, and they were my own sobs . . . I stopped, halfway up the spiral staircase, in almost total darkness, just enough light coming through the tiny slit windows to give a vague outline of the staircase. I was stunned to find myself there. There were salty trails of wetness on my cheeks. I was tensed, waiting for the noise that failed to materialize: a loud, sharp explosion that I knew now had been a gun shot. There was no gun shot now, just the steady pad of footsteps crossing the floor of the library below.

Wiping the tears from my cheeks, gaining a shaky composure, I went on up the staircase. On the second landing, I groped for the knob and pressed it. The wall swung outward, revealing the shadowy, sagging gallery.

I moved very slowly, very carefully, each step cautiously placed on the warped, rotten floorboards. It wasn't going to tear away from the wall. I was certain of that. It had supported the weight of both of us that morning. No matter how it swayed, no matter how it creaked and protested, it would hold. I told myself that with great confidence. Nevertheless, I was absolutely terrified. I could feel the panic threatening. My throat was dry. My legs trembled. Waves of dizziness swept over me, and I leaned back against the wall of decaying books. *Don't look down, Jane. Don't look down.* But I couldn't help myself. Something compelled me to peer over the railing at the floor three stories below. So far down . . . so very far. I closed my eyes, realizing my folly. I must have been out of my mind, out of my mind . . .

There had been lamps burning that night, warm yellow light that burnished leather bindings and picked out gilt lettering. The floorboards had been sturdy beneath my bare feet as I scurried along in that absurdly long flannel nightgown. I had to hide the necklace. Mother told me to hide it. Uncle

Charles wanted to steal it, and something was wrong. Something was dreadfully wrong. Mother had been crying as she rushed out into the hall, and those angry voices had shouted and raged in some distant room. "Charles will kill him! He has a gun!" she had cried, and I knew what that explosion had been. Uncle Charles had killed Daddy, and he wanted the necklace . . .

I forced myself to move. Leaning against the books, I edged my way along, inch by inch. There was the hole Brence had made, jagged splinters of wood hanging down, torn, shattered books surrounding it. The air was thick with dust, and every movement I made stirred up more. The platform sagged, creaking, seeming to pull away from the wall, but somehow I forced myself to go on.

Gibbon. *The Decline and Fall of the Roman Empire.* I remembered that title, and I could see the books in my mind, a set of six, bound in tan and brown leather. Where? Further along. I could never locate them in this position, back against the wall. Steeling myself, I moved away from the books and closer to the railing so that I could read the titles as I went. A horrible tearing noise rent the air. The gallery tilted, the floor slanting down and out like the deck of a ship dipping in the water. The slant was no more than two inches, but it seemed I would surely slip and fall crashing against the fragile railing. It would snap in two like dry matchsticks. I would go hurtling through space . . . No, no, I mustn't think about it. I must remain calm. Steady. Weight balanced, no sudden movements.

The books were on the fourth shelf, their titles almost obscured by thick layers of dust. I had to bend down to pull them out, but they had been at shoulder height then . . . I pulled them out and hid the necklace behind them and pushed them back in place, and then I heard footsteps in the hall, running, high heels clattering on the parquet, and I knew it was my mother. She came rushing into the library, her long blonde curls spilling in every direction, the elegant black lace on her blue satin dinner gown torn, one sleeve of the gown ripped away. She pushed against the doors, trying to close them, but the doors flew back, knocking her down. He stood over her, his face contorted with fury. "Where is it!" he yelled, and she crawled away from him, on the carpet, cringing. He seized her arm and pulled her to her feet and struck her face, again, again, again. She was screaming now, and I was screaming, too, but they couldn't hear me. They didn't know I was there. "Tell me!" he shouted. Her face was bruised, her cheek bleeding, and he seized her throat and shook her. Her arms waved in the air and she fell to her knees and he was still shaking her. Mother was a rag doll, limp, and when he let go of her she dropped in a jumbled heap, her head at such a funny angle. I made no sound. I was still screaming, but the screams were all trapped inside. He stared down at her, and then he picked her up and slung her over his shoulder and took her away, and I stayed there all night, still screaming. I heard the low rumble. The house seemed to shake. There was a great crash, then another and another. It was morning when I crept down the staircase and back to my room, and when Uncle Charles came in looking grave and upset I just stared at him, wondering why he had come into my room instead of my mother, wondering what he was talking about, what accident...

I pulled the books off the shelf. They crumbled, bindings splitting, pages falling loose. Reaching into the space, I felt the hard stones and pulled them out. The necklace was heavy in my hands, the diamonds yellow with dust. I stared at it numbly, tears in my eyes. The gallery sagged again, and there was a splitting, ripping noise. I paid no attention. I looked at the cursed, dust-dimmed jewels in my hand, thinking of all the tragedy they had brought.

"You've found them," Charles Danver said.

I turned very slowly and looked at him. He had only come a short way along the gallery, not more than ten feet, and he stood very still, his face white, a streak of dust across one cheek.

"Bring them to me, Jane," he commanded.

"No," I said calmly.

"If I have to come after them we'll both be killed. It won't hold the weight of both of us."

"I'm not afraid," I replied.

It was true. I wasn't afraid. I had just lived through a nightmare of stark terror, and it had left me numb. I gazed at Charles Danver with calm, level eyes, and I knew this wasn't really happening. This was just a continuation of the nightmare. Jane was far away. She was observing all this with cool objectivity. The girl who stood on the tilting gallery was someone else, a girl in a dream.

"You followed me," I said.

He nodded. "I went directly to your room as soon as I came home. I had to find out how much Helene had told you. You were gone. I heard you walking down the back hall."

"Where is Susie?"

"I've no idea. We're quite alone in the house."

"You murdered Madame DuBois."

"I broke her neck yesterday morning, a few minutes after I left you in the study. I had my arm crooked around her throat while she wrote the note. As soon as she finished I applied a bit more pressure. She struggled violently, the bitch. I'm afraid it was extremely painful for her."

"You murdered my mother, too. I saw. I was here, in this room. I saw everything. I know what happened that night. You shot Daddy—"

"He was being very unreasonable. I shot him, yes. I didn't intend to murder Jeanne. I only meant to frighten her into telling me what she'd done with the diamonds. I got rather carried away—didn't know my own strength. She died on me—" He shook his head, a thoughtful look in his eyes. "I had two bodies on my hands. I had to dispose of them some way. I dragged them into the west wing. I'd worked in a coal mine for a spell, knew all about dynamite, knew George kept some in a shed at the mill. It was quite simple. No one ever questioned the authenticity of the 'accident.' People assumed the wing just collapsed."

"She knew, though."

"Helene? She was my accomplice—my willing slave. It wasn't difficult to persuade her to help me arrange the accident. She also provided my alibi. She testified I was in my own room in the east wing, fast asleep when the tragedy occurred. There were no other servants in the house that night, and Brence had gone chasing after some village lass, didn't come back until it was all over."

"She helped you look for the necklace."

"For eleven years. We finally decided it was buried somewhere in the rubble. I had to maintain my position at the mill. I couldn't be seen digging around in broad daylight. We searched at night."

"You were there when I—"

"I hit you on the head with a rock," he said simply.

"You sent for me because you thought—"

"I knew you'd lost any memory of Danver Hall. I hoped bringing you back would help you remember. I thought perhaps you might know something about the necklace. It was a gamble, but it's paid off, hasn't it? Bring it to me, Jane."

"No."

"I won't hurt you."

"You'll have to come get it."

"Be reasonable, Jane."

I held up the necklace, dangling it. Even under the dust, even in that faint, fading light there was some glitter left. Charles Danver cursed as he took a few steps forward, his face tight with terror. There was another tearing noise. He flattened himself against the books, his chest heaving. His forehead was beaded with sweat. I smiled without knowing why. He began to edge along the wall, dust sprinkling down over his fine suit. Several books tumbled out of the shelves, falling apart as they hit the floor.

"You're very heavy," I said calmly. "It'll probably give way any moment now."

"Damn you!"

"The mighty Charles Danver is finally afraid."

He ignored me. He had moved past the gaping hole now. He was perhaps twenty feet away from me. His face was the color of putty, and the corners of his mouth trembled. Flattened against the wall, his palms gripping the shelves, he slid along slowly. His breath came in heavy gasps. The gallery rocked and sagged, the tearing noise one continuous shriek now. He closed his eyes, halting abruptly, too terrified to go on. Several minutes passed as he tried to master his fear. I could almost see his strength returning. His tensed muscles relaxed. Color returned to his face. He turned his head to stare at me with eyes glowing with fierce determination.

"Tell me about Jamintha," I said.

"You know her name?"

"I know everything about her. You were with her this afternoon."

He frowned, puzzled by my knowledge. He was still flattened against the wall, storing up his strength.

"She wasn't there when I woke up," he said, the frown deepening. "I don't know where she went. I came back here—"

"You love her," I said.

"Finding the necklace has changed everything," he said ponderously. "Brence can have the mill. I won't have to bother with it any longer. The diamonds—a fortune—" He was talking to himself now, looking into a future of staggering wealth. "I'm going to take her away from here. I may even marry her."

He took a deep breath. With great caution, he turned around until he was facing me, his right shoulder touching the wall. He came toward me, each step causing the floor to wobble vigorously. His mouth was spread in a tight line. His brows were lowered. His eyes were like dark burning coals. He came nearer, and nearer, ignoring the danger now, oblivious to it.

I stared at him, and suddenly the dream-like

trance was broken, that curious objectivity shattering. The look in his eyes jolted me into reality, a terrifying, incredible reality. He intended to kill me. I tried to cry out, but no sound would come. I stepped back, my legs so weak that I almost fell. He smiled, relishing my fear, enjoying it.

"No—" I whispered hoarsely.

"You're going to die," he promised.

"No—Jamintha! Jamintha!" I cried. "Help me. Help me!"

I closed my eyes, sobbing. I trembled, my body seized by a strange convulsion. Blood and bone and muscle were frozen in the darkness, and then warmth came, and I opened my eyes. Dropping the necklace into the pocket of my dress, I removed the pins from my hair and shook the braids loose. Jane was gone. Jane was asleep. Rich chestnut locks tumbled to my shoulders, and I smiled at him, my eyes full of mockery.

"My God!" he whispered. "My God in Heaven—"

I took the necklace from my pocket and held it out, dangling it in front of him.

"You want it, Charles? Take it."

In one part of my mind I was aware of the shouts below, aware of the loud footsteps ringing on the tower staircase, but I paid no attention to the noise. I swung the necklace to and fro, watching the incredulous expression on his face. He was stunned, shocked into immobility, but only for a moment. He reached for the necklace. I dangled it over the railing. He leaned forward, seizing it. He cried out as the weight of his body caused him to topple against the rotten wooden railing. The railing snapped with a brittle popping sound, and his scream seemed to last for a long time before the dull thud terminated it.

I leaned back against the shelves, staring at that gaping hole in the railing. Someone was calling my name. I turned to see Brence edging toward me. Gavin stood just inside the tower, and I could see Susie behind him.

"Brence—" I moaned.

"Easy," he said, "easy. We've done this before. There's no need to be afraid. Reach your hand out, Jane. Be calm. Be very calm. Don't look down."

"What happened? Brence, what *happened?*"

And then he took my hand.

CHAPTER SIXTEEN

The August sun was hot, but shimmering heat waves could not deter the vacationers who waited all year round for their two weeks by the water. Children played gaily on the beach, rushing to splash in the foamy waves, and women in light colored dresses reclined under the shade of enormous umbrellas. Men in conservative suits and tight collars watched with proud, self-satisfied expressions. The water was a vivid blue, purple on the horizon, and beyond the esplanade ornate hotels and grand shops glittered in the direct sunlight. I had been here in Brighton for over eight months, but this was the first time I had taken a stroll by myself.

Gavin had always been with me before.

I loved the beach. I loved the salty spray and the screaming children and the festive atmosphere. I watched as a large brown dog loped after the ball tossed by a grubby little boy in a blue sailor suit. I smiled as the ball bounced in the water and the dog

JAMINTHA

leaped after it. How beautiful life could be, how pleasant and uncomplicated. Simple things could bring great joy. Life itself was a wondrous miracle, a gift we must cherish and savor to the full. It was wonderful to be alive, to be attune to life, to respond to it without fear.

Gavin had accomplished wonders during these eight months, eight months of "therapy"—a new word—of long, long talks and memory sessions in the white frame clinic with blue shutters and spacious, sun-filled rooms. I was a willing patient, and now . . . and now I was cured. The blind boy could see again. Prim, thorny Jane Danver was gone forever, and so was Jamintha, her other extreme.

Who remained?

A third me, the me I might have been had I not suffered the shock of that night eleven—almost twelve—years ago. I had neither Jane's stiff demeanor nor Jamintha's flamboyant verve, Jane's timidity nor Jamintha's boldness. I was still Jane, but new, a new person. It was a glorious sensation, like waking up after a long sleep to find a room full of presents. I understood it all now. I had discovered it for myself. Gavin had guided me, but he had never explained.

I sat down on a white wooden bench to watch the rushing blue waves and the children playing and the gulls fluttering like bits of white confetti against the sky. I allowed myself to think about that afternoon eight months ago.

Had it not been for Susie, I might not be here today. She had gone to my room that afternoon to check on me. She found it empty. (I was Jamintha then. I was at the cottage, serving brandy to Charles Danver, listening to his confession of murder.) Alarmed, Susie searched the house, growing more and more frantic. Finally she rushed out to saddle one of the horses and rode to the mill to tell Brence. He was in his father's office talking to Gavin, who had just returned from London and was trying to convince him how imperative it was that I be given immediate care. Suspecting the truth, Gavin had gone to the city to interview the staff of my school, to track down and question all the doctors who had examined me during those years. He was convinced that I was schizophrenic, that I was in grave danger of a complete mental collapse. Brence thought the man was out of his mind. And then Susie had burst in on them and they had come racing back to the house, arriving just in time to hear the shrill tearing noises in the library.

Charles Danver was dead. He had fallen to his death, his hand clutching the necklace that had obsessed him for eleven years. How ironic it all was, I thought. The diamonds, those glittering stars, were fake, an exquisite imitation. The necklace was a copy of the original that one of the de Soissons had probably sold a century before, and there was no proof that it wasn't a copy of some other necklace. Marie Antoinette's diamonds had disappeared. The mystery would never be solved.

When Brence agreed that it would be best if I left Danver Hall immediately, Gavin brought me here to Brighton, to the unpretentious little clinic run by one of his friends. Eight months of mending, eight months of anguish and frustration and rebellion and tears, and finally that light breaking over the horizon of my mind, awareness, understanding, rebirth.

"Jamintha, my little Jamintha." That was her

pet name for me. I was her little Jane, her Jamintha. I had loved her so. I had wanted to be exactly like her. Witnessing her death had been a brutal shock. That shock had created the schism inside of me. Jamintha, the bright, merry, irrepressible little girl had vanished, and a stunned, uncomprehending, almost catatonic Jane had been sent away to school. But Jamintha wasn't gone. During times of stress, she took over, she left dull Jane in her bed and slipped over the wall to meet the delivery boy. She led a gay, frivolous, existence while Jane suffered from headaches and inexplicable exhaustion. Jane *knew* about Jamintha, but Jamintha was a separate personality, completely disassociated from Jane. Jamintha was like my mother, like *her* mother. During those long years at school, Jamintha appeared, not often, perhaps, but always when the unhappiness and the dreary brown atmosphere and the taunts and ridicule became too much for Jane to bear.

And then I had come to Danver Hall . . .

The stress had been even greater than it had been at school, and the blow on the head I had received in the ruined west wing had released Jamintha, giving her a freedom she had never had before. She was fully alive, overjoyed at the release. She needed money, so she stole Madame DuBois' carefully saved pin money, and that enabled her to rent the cottage and buy new clothes. Jane's drab dresses would never do. She kept her finery in the huge old wardrobe in the back hall, carefully locked away, the key hidden under a stack of linen handkerchiefs in Jane's room. During the afternoons when Jane was closed up in her room, asleep, Jamintha lived the life Jane would never have dared. Later, when she returned, she sat at Jane's desk and composed her letters.

I knew it was all true. The key had been in my drawer, the dresses in the wardrobe, and the stationery Jamintha had used was hidden in the bottom drawer of the bureau. I accepted it all, but there were still so many questions that had needed to be answered.

The handwriting? Why hadn't I recognized it?

"*Jamintha* wrote those letters," Gavin said, "Jane didn't. A person's handwriting reveals a great deal about her personality. Yours—Jane's—is small, neat, compact, stiff and formal. Jamintha's is—was—dashing and gay, embellished with loops and curliques and dashes. *You* didn't write those letters, Jane. She did."

"How could I—how could Jamintha have gotten in and out of the house without anyone seeing her? Most of the time it was broad daylight. Someone *must* have seen her."

"I'll let you figure that one out," Gavin replied.

"It seems impossible," I said. "Unless—"

"Yes?"

"She used the secret passage."

He had nodded, pleased with me. Now, sitting on the sun-warmed bench and watching the waves rushing over the sand, I thought about Gavin Clark. From the very beginning, he had suspected Jamintha. At first he thought she was merely a figment of my imagination, like the imaginary friends lonely children often create for playmates. Later, in the village, he had actually seen her, and she looked very familiar. This puzzled him, and he began to suspect the truth. Cases of double personality were rare, extremely rare, but they were not unheard of. Stevenson had based his *Dr. Jekyll and Mr. Hyde* on such a case. Gavin began to ask me leading questions, and then when I had told him about the secret passage and shown him the bruises on my forearms—the bruises Brence had given me—he was almost certain. He had left for London immediately to talk to the school staff and the doctors, and although none of them had been aware of the truth, their statements and comments about me had verified it for Gavin.

He had been so wonderful during these past eight months, so patient. I thought about that quiet, firm voice, those remarkable brown eyes in the lined, weary face. Every day we had talked. Every day he had taken valuable time away from his book in order to work with me. I sat in the comfortable old leather chair, and Gavin usually paced the room, pausing now and then to jot something down in his notebook, his rich, melodious voice soothing me. He made me see. He made me understand. The schism was mended, and Jamintha would never return. Neither would Jane, the Jane who had found life so frightening and bleak.

The thing that had puzzled me more than anything else was how Jamintha could have deceived both Brence and Charles Danver. Why hadn't they recognized her? Why hadn't they known immediately that Jamintha was really Jane? Gavin had an answer for that, too.

"There were great external differences, of course. Jane was pale, her hair worn in tight severe braids. Jamintha's complexion glowed with health, her hair falling loose in rich waves. Jane wore drab, simple dresses that made her look even plainer. Jamintha wore bright silks that heightened her color, dresses cut to reveal her figure. That in itself might not have been enough to deceive most people, but there was an even greater difference. Jane was quiet, withdrawing, meek. Jamintha was animated, vivacious, dazzling. The physical features were the same, true, but only in the essentials of shape and form. Jane's face was unremarkable, the beauty dimmed, almost effaced by pallor and a prim expression, eyes downcast, mouth tight. Jamintha was lit by an inner glow, her eyes sparkling, her cheeks flushed a vivid pink, her mouth smiling. She looked different because she *was* different."

And what remained? Jamintha's dazzling beauty was gone, but so were Jane's severe braids and prim expression. My hair fell in long waves, fastened behind each temple with a white ribbon. I wore a white muslin dress sprigged with tiny blue and green flowers, the square neckline cut low because of the summer heat, the short sleeves puffed. I was a pretty girl, neither beautiful nor plain, a girl like any other, nineteen years old, sitting on a bench by the seashore. I was Jane, and Jamintha, and someone new—serene, calm, slightly pensive.

Lost in thought, I had been unaware of the passage of time. The beach was deserted, laughing children vanished, languid ladies and proud fathers long since retired to the hotels. The tall umbrellas cast long shadows over the wet sand, and already a cool evening breeze had sprung up. It would be dark before long. I should get back to the clinic. Gavin would be worried about me . . . for entirely different reasons now.

He was in love with me. I knew that instinctively. He looked at me with tender eyes, and he smiled in a new way, and his manner was protective and gentle and . . . and he loved me. He would ask me to marry him soon. I knew that, too. He would be a wonderful husband. He was handsome and intelligent and kind. He would cherish me. He would always be there, always dependable, always thoughtful, sharing himself, his work, his ambition, his emotions. With Gavin, life would be comfortable. It would be satisfying, rich with intimacy and warmth. He was everything a woman could want, more than most women could ever hope for. Why, then, did I dread that question I knew would come?

I was fond of him. I admired him. I was grateful to him, but . . . but I didn't love him. I couldn't marry him. He deserved a love as rare and unselfish as his own, and I couldn't provide that. There was room in my heart for only one . . . *No, Jane, don't start thinking about that. You've accepted it. You've resigned yourself to it. There's no need to think about him, to wonder, to nourish this foolish hope.*

I got up and started walking slowly along the beach. To my right, beyond the beach and the wide street, the hotels were spangled with gold and silver lights, and I could hear music drifting out from one of the ballrooms. The breeze fluttered my hair. My light muslin skirt billowed. He hadn't come to see me. He hadn't written. He hadn't shown the least sign of interest. He was busy, of course. The mill must keep him fully occupied. After eight months he must have initiated all those changes he'd been talking about. He had no time for anything else, probably, and . . . and it was foolish to dwell on it. That part of my life was over. I must think about the future.

I could become a teacher, perhaps, or perhaps I could be a governess. Recently, I had been helping Gavin with his book, keeping his files in order, transcribing notes, doing some background work. Perhaps I could become a secretary, or . . . or a librarian. A few women were being hired in these positions, although it was still highly unconventional. I would find a job. I would support myself. I would savor the miracle of life and enjoy all the blessings most people took for granted. I would try to forget him, and perhaps someday I would succeed.

I saw the man walking toward me. He was far away, a distant silhouette moving in my direction. I paid no attention at first. As he drew nearer, I stopped, staring at him, and I knew it couldn't be true. I knew it couldn't be him. It couldn't be Brence.

It was.

"The good doctor is worried," he said lazily. "He was getting ready to come looking for you when I arrived. I told him I'd find you and I have . . . Hello, Jane."

"Hello, Brence."

"It's been a long time."

"Yes."

"You're looking—very well."

"Thank you."

So stiff. So formal. So awkward.

"Why did you come?" I inquired.

"He sent for me. I told him to let me know the minute you were—uh—the minute you were—well, cured, I suppose. Every week he sent a report on your progress. He kept me well informed. Day before yesterday he sent a letter saying you were—ready."

"Ready for what?"

"Ready to come back," he said simply.

"I'm not going back, Brence."

"Did you know the good doctor is in love with you?" he asked, ignoring my comment. "It's as plain as the nose on his face. He wants to marry you. I asked him about it just now. He said he loved you, and you know what I said?"

"What?"

"I said may the best man win."

I made no comment. I didn't trust myself to say anything.

"I've changed, too," he said. "That night, when I was fifteen years old, I saw the west wing collapse, and I saw my father standing out in the yard, watching it. The look on his face—I knew. DuBois told everyone he was asleep at the time. I *knew*, but I refused to acknowledge it. I almost told you about it that day in the woods when we were having the picnic. I'd wanted to tell someone for such a long time—" He paused, a pained expression on his handsome face. "I knew my father was a murderer. Deep down I knew, and it tormented me. It—well, I drank and caroused. I got into fights. I threw tantrums. And all the time I was trying to run away from that knowledge, that fact I couldn't accept. It wasn't very admirable of me, and I wasn't a very admirable chap. All those things you said about me were true. I've tried to make amends, Jane."

"Have you?"

"I've worked hard. I've initiated a lot of changes at the mill. I've worked right alongside the men many a time. And I haven't touched a drop of liquor—though God knows there've been times when I was sorely tempted. I think you could respect me now. I think you could even love me, Jane. I'm a damned good bargain."

"Are you?"

"Sure," he replied. His voice was light and jaunty now. "I'm rich and devilishly good looking and thoroughly reformed. And I love you. We're going to be married."

"You loved Jamintha."

"I sure as hell did."

"Jamintha is gone, Brence. She'll never return."

"Who needs her?" he said flippantly.

"Brence—"

"I love *you*, wench."

"How could you? You don't—"

"Look, I still have a bad temper. I'm about to lose it. Let's not argue. I've built a fine new house on the edge of town. It's a grand place, and it's waiting for you. Danver Hall can sink into the bog for all I care, but the new house—I built it for you, Jane. Susie's been keeping house for me, but that damned Johnny Stone's been after her to marry him and the minx is going to abandon me. I *need* you."

"To keep house for you? No, thank you. You can find some—"

He swung me into his arms. He kissed me for a long, long time there on the wet beach with the waves slapping the sand. His arms held me tightly against him, and his mouth worked hard on mine, and all the strength and resolution left me and I clung to him. He released me and jammed his hands into his trouser pockets and looked at me with an infuriating grin.

"Convinced?" he said.

"I—I don't know."

He scowled. He reached out for me again. The second kiss was even more persuasive than the first. I rubbed my hands over his back, feeling hard muscle beneath the silk. Still holding me, he drew his head back and looked down into my eyes.

"I intend to have you," he said gruffly, "and I'm going to keep right on kissing you until you give in. Shall we try it again?"

"By all means," I said.

GOTHIC MYSTERIES
of Romance and Suspense...

by Rae Foley
- [ ] FATAL LADY — 75¢
- [ ] THE FIRST MRS. WINSTON — 95¢
- [ ] GIRLS FROM NOWHERE — 95¢
- [ ] RUN FOR YOUR LIFE — 75¢
- [ ] SLEEP WITHOUT MORNING — 75¢
- [ ] TRUST A WOMAN — 95¢

by Mary Westmacott
- [ ] ABSENT IN THE SPRING — 75¢
- [ ] THE BURDEN — 75¢
- [ ] A DAUGHTER'S A DAUGHTER — 75¢
- [ ] GIANT'S BREAD — 75¢

Buy them at your local bookstore or use this handy coupon for ordering:

Dell DELL BOOKS
P.O. BOX 1000, PINEBROOK, N.J. 07058

Please send me the books I have checked above. I am enclosing $_____ (please add 25¢ per copy to cover postage and handling). Send check or money order—no cash or C.O.D.'s.

Mr/Mrs/Miss_____

Address_____

City_____ State/Zip_____

*Foreboding mansions,
moonlight and the moaning wind
... a setting for romance,
intrigue and the supernatural*

GOTHIC MYSTERIES

☐	CAPE HOUSE *L. P. Shepherd*	95¢
☐	THE BOXWOOD MAZE *Bentz Plagemann*	95¢
☐	CAMERON HILL *Mary Kay Simmons*	75¢
☐	A CANDLE FOR THE DRAGON *Mary Craig*	75¢
☐	DARK INTERVAL *Joan Aiken*	75¢
☐	THE DARK SONATA *Beatrice Murray*	75¢
☐	BORROWER OF THE NIGHT *Elizabeth Peters*	95¢
☐	EVIL THAT WALKS INVISIBLE *Alicen White*	75¢
☐	THE FORBIDDEN TOWER *Eugenia Cook*	75¢
☐	THE HOUSE OF KURAGIN *Constance Heaven*	1.50
☐	THE HOUSE CALLED EDENHYTHE *Nancy Buckingham*	75¢
☐	IT'S DIFFERENT ABROAD *Henry Calvin*	1.95
☐	THE LEDGE *Gertrude Schweitzer*	75¢
☐	MASQUERADE IN VENICE *Velda Johnston*	1.25
☐	MIRANDA *Jane Blackmore*	75¢
☐	THE ROOM UPSTAIRS *Mildred Davis*	1.25
☐	TEARS IN PARADISE *Jane Blackmore*	95¢
☐	THE VENGEANCE OF VALDONE *Betty Fern*	75¢

Buy them at your local bookstore or use this handy coupon for ordering:

Dell **DELL BOOKS**
P.O. BOX 1000, PINEBROOK, N.J. 07058

Please send me the books I have checked above. I am enclosing $_____
(please add 25¢ per copy to cover postage and handling). Send check or money order—no cash or C.O.D.'s.

Mr/Mrs/Miss_____

Address_____

City_____ State/Zip_____

Castlemore

A Novel by

Charles MacKinnon

CHRISTMAS, 1906. Edwardian England dominated the world, peace and prosperity ruled the land, and at the proud mansion of Castlemore, the MacInnes family gathered for its annual reunion.

This stirring romantic chronicle, written by the present Laird of Dunakin, traces the lives and loves, in peace and in war, of three generations of a grand Scottish family, the Clan MacInnes. Spanning the years between the turn of the century and the Second World War, CASTLEMORE is an enthralling evocation of another romantic time.

"... Heartfelt and moving ..."
—*Publishers Weekly*

A DELL BOOK $1.50

At your local bookstore or use this handy coupon for ordering:

Dell | **DELL BOOKS** | CASTLEMORE $1.50
P.O. BOX 1000, PINEBROOK, N.J. 07058

Please send me the above title. I am enclosing $_____
(please add 25¢ per copy to cover postage and handling). Send check or money order—no cash or C.O.D.'s.

Mr/Mrs/Miss_____

Address_____

City_____ State/Zip_____

This offer expires 6/75